THEMATIC UNIT

Our Country

Written by Cynthia Holzschuher, M. Ed.

Teacher Created Materials, Inc.
6421 Industry Way
Westminster, CA 92683
www.teachercreated.com
©2002 Teacher Created Materials, Inc.
Made in U.S.A.
ISBN-0-7439-3104-1

Edited by
Melissa Hart, M.F.A.

Illustrated by
Renée Christine Yates

Cover Art by
Kevin Barnes

Table of Contents

Introduction

Our Country is a thematic literature unit which gives students the opportunity to learn more about America's presidents, national symbols, and historical monuments. Within these 80 pages, teachers will find lesson ideas and reproducible pages designed to use with intermediate-aged students. Four high quality nonfiction picture books—*So You Want to Be President?*, *Eyewitness: Presidents*, *Uncle Sam and Old Glory*, and *A is for America*—provide the basis for these materials. Teachers will find introductory and supplemental activities that encourage and extend the reading of each title. Additional activities provide curriculum connections to language arts, math, science, social studies, art, music, and life skills. The unit ends with bulletin board ideas and culminating activities.

This thematic unit includes the following:

☆ **Literature selections**—summaries of four children's books with related lessons and reproducible pages

☆ **Planning Guides**—suggestions for sequencing lessons during each day of the unit

☆ **Writing Ideas**—poetry and writing suggestions for writing across the curriculum

☆ **Extensions**—additional ideas to accommodate a variety of performance levels and learning styles

☆ **Curriculum Connections**—activities in language arts, math, science, social studies, art, and music

☆ **Group Projects**—activities to foster small group, cooperative learning

☆ **Bulletin Board Ideas**—suggestions and clip art for student-created and/or interactive bulletin boards

☆ **Culminating Activities**—ideas which require students to synthesize their learning by engaging in activities to share with others

☆ **Bibliography**—a list of additional books and websites on the themes explored in *Our Country*.

To keep this resource intact so that it may be used year after year, you may wish to punch holes in the pages and store them in a three-ring binder.

Introduction (cont.)

Why Balance Basic Skills and Whole Language?

The strength of a whole language approach involves children using several modes of communication—reading, writing, listening, observing, illustrating, and speaking. Communication skills are integrated into lessons that emphasize the whole of language. Balancing this approach is our knowledge that every whole—including individual words—is composed of parts, and directed study of those parts can help a student master the whole. Experience and research tell us that regular attention to phonics, other word-attack skills, spelling, etc., develops reading mastery, thereby completing the unity of the whole language experience. The child is thus led to read, write, spell, speak, listen, and think in response to a literature experience introduced by the teacher. In these ways language skills grow rapidly, stimulated by direct practice, involvement, and interest in the topic at hand.

Why Thematic Planning?

One useful tool for implementing an integrated whole language program is thematic planning. By choosing a theme with corresponding literature selections for a unit of study, a teacher can plan activities throughout the day that lead to cohesive, in-depth study of the topic. Students practice and apply their skills in meaningful contexts. Consequently, they learn and retain more. Both teachers and students are freed from a day that is broken into unrelated segments of isolated drill and practice.

Why Journals?

Each day your students should have the opportunity to write in their journals. They may respond to a book, write about a personal experience, or answer a general "question of the day" posed by you. Students should be encouraged to refer to the posted vocabulary list to check their spelling. You may read journals every day or choose to alternate days. The cumulative journal provides an excellent means of documenting writing progress.

Why Technology?

Our students are living in a world where use of technology is imperative. In order to compete successfully outside the classroom, they must engage in a wide range of technological experiences, including word-processing and use of the Internet. Technology helps to motivate students and enhance the learning process by providing another avenue by which to gain and report information.

So You Want to Be President?

by Judith St. George

This 2001 Caldecott Medal-winning book contains a collection of facts and anecdotes about the lives and times of the U.S. presidents. Pictured as cartoon style caricatures, the presidents are cleverly grouped to show their personality traits, interests, and peculiarities in order to underscore the theme that anyone can be president regardless of size, income, age, family, or education. A factual addendum at the back provides names and dates, offering a one-line biography for each past president.

Eyewitness: Presidents

by James Barber

This is an excellent introduction to the presidents of the United States. Each entry features a brief summary text as well as photos, maps, documents, captions, and sidebars explaining historical and personal events. As an accurate research tool, it also includes information about scandals and negative press described in a manner appropriate for children.

Sample Plan

Lesson I
- Compare the covers and pictures in both books.
- Distribute "Mount Rushmore" (page 10).
- Distribute "A Day in the Life of the President" (page 41).
- Complete a daily writing topic (page 47) about the duties/requirements of the presidency.
- Begin the presidential map.

Lesson II
- Share *So You Want to Be President?* Try to identify the presidents from their caricatures.
- Begin a wall chart of descriptive words for presidents; distribute page 45.
- Work in groups to write presidential brain teasers or riddles.
- Begin an illustrated presidential time line.
- Write an opinion paragraph using a daily writing topic (page 47).

Lesson III
- Share pages 4–23 of *Eyewitness: Presidents.*
- Add the presidents (1–15) to your time line.
- Complete "George Washington" (page 12) and "Thomas Jefferson" (page 13).
- Distribute "The Money Makers. U. S. Mint" (page 52) and play the game.
- Complete presidential averages (page 50).

Lesson IV
- Share pages 24–41 of *Eyewitness: Presidents.*
- Add the presidents (16–31) to the time line.
- Complete "Abraham Lincoln" (page 14).
- Share *Lincoln: A Photo-biography* by Russell Freedman or other presidential biographies.

Lesson V
- Share pages 42–64 of *Eyewitness: Presidents.*
- Add the presidents (32–current) to the time line.
- Complete "Franklin Delano Roosevelt" (page 15).
- Complete "Presidential Epitaphs" (page 42).
- Complete "Patriots and Patriotism" (page 38).

Lesson VI
- Do research on the presidents' cabinet members and the first ladies.
- Complete "Getting Personal with Presidents" on page 11 for the president of your choice.
- Complete all activities on Washington, D.C., including "The National Mall" (page 43), "Be a Washington Meterorlogist" (page 58), "Branches of Government" (page 60), and "Washington, D.C., Logic Puzzle" (page 54).

Overview of Activities

Setting the Stage

1. Compare the pictures in both books. Ask students which style they prefer and why. Explain that the cover of *So You Want to Be President?* depicts Mount Rushmore, a sculpture in the Black Hills of South Dakota. Distribute copies of "Mount Rushmore" on page 10.

2. Make available a variety of presidential biographies at several different reading levels. Encourage students to read independently while they complete the work in this unit.

3. Distribute copies of "A Day in the Life of the President" on page 41 and brainstorm a list of specific presidential duties that are not mentioned in the activity. Complete a daily writing topic (page 47) about the duties/requirements of the president. Ask students to suggest at least one other requirement that would be appropriate to ask of a president. Other discussion topics might include: What are the pros and cons of being the president? or How is a president like/unlike a king?

4. Prepare the Presidential Birthplace Bulletin Board on page 73. The map bulletin boards will function as interactive learning tools throughout the unit.

Enjoying the Book(s)

1. Share *So You Want to Be President?* This book won the Caldecott Medal (2001). Ask students to explain what they like/dislike about the illustrations. Discuss why caricatures are appropriate for the style of the text. If possible, share other examples of caricatures (i.e., political or editorial cartoons from the newspaper).

2. Begin a wall chart of descriptive words for presidents, and distribute page 45. Continue building a descriptive word bank throughout the unit. Display it in a prominent place in your classroom so that it may be referred to for writing assignments.

3. Brainstorm examples of how the information in the book could be used for riddles or brain teasers (e.g., "Which president didn't go to college?"). Ask students to write one original riddle and answer on a slip of paper and drop it in a container. Take a few minutes to read and answer the riddles. Another day, ask students to write and illustrate their brain teaser ideas, then combine the pages in a class book. Distribute copies of "Getting Personal with Presidents" on page 11.

4. Ask students to write a paragraph explaining their opinion of this book. Did they enjoy the illustrations? humor? trivia? Be sure they support their opinions with clear examples.

5. Begin an illustrated time line of presidents using the pictures on pages 75 and 76, as well as the information at the back of *So You Want to Be President?* and *Eyewitness: Presidents*. You may choose to complete the time line in three sections to complement reading (see #6).

6. Share *Eyewitness: Presidents* in three sections: I. pages 4–23 (Washington—Buchanan), II. pages 24–41 (Lincoln—Hoover), and III. pages 42–63 (Franklin Roosevelt—Clinton). Add each president to the time line as you read/discuss him. Use "Presidential Faces" on pages 75–76 and include a few facts about each man or about the events that occurred during his administration.

Overview of Activities *(cont.)*

=== **Enjoying the Book(s)** *(cont.)* ===

7. Have students complete one activity sheet for each section of reading: I. George Washington on page 12, II. Thomas Jefferson on page 13, III. Abraham Lincoln on page 14, and IV. Franklin Delano Roosevelt on page 15. The format of these sheets includes vocabulary words, comprehension questions, and extended activities.

8. Share biographies of other presidents, particularly *Lincoln: A Photo-biography* by Russell Freedman (Scott Foresman, 1989). This Newbery Medal-winning book presents a fascinating account of Lincoln's life and career. Encourage students to select one president for independent study and complete "Getting Personal with Presidents" (page 11).

=== **Extending the Book(s)** ===

1. Complete all the activities on "The National Mall" on page 43, "Be a Washington Meteorologist" on page 58, "Branches of Government" on page 60, and "Washington, D.C., Logic Puzzle" on page 54.

2. Students may search the Internet or an encyclopedia for information about the history of our capitol.

3. Ask your class to think of a current problem that involves federal laws. Discuss what the president is doing to address the problem and ask students to explain what they might do differently. Ask students to bring newspaper articles on the subject to class and complete a current events summary on page 64 as a homework assignment.

4. Who helps the president make decisions? Assign small groups to design a wall chart showing the various positions in the president's cabinet. They may also include the names of current cabinet members and a brief explanation of their responsibilities.

5. Discuss the position and duties of the first lady. Have each student select a first lady to research, then write a brief paper highlighting her contributions to the United States. Students may search encyclopedias, books, and the Internet for useful information.

Presidential Name Game

Over the centuries, U.S. presidents have often shared the same first names. Many of the first presidents were named after people in the Bible or after British kings. Some later presidents were named for those men who had previously served as president of the United States.

Activity

Complete this page by adding the last names to the first names of these presidents.

James

1. _____
2. _____
3. _____
4. _____
5. _____
6. _____

Andrew

1. _____
2. _____

John

1. _____
2. _____
3. _____
4. _____

George

1. _____
2. _____
3. _____

William

1. _____
2. _____
3. _____
4. _____

Franklin

1. _____
2. _____

Extended Activity

☆ Research your own name in the dictionary or on the Internet. What does your name mean? For whom were you named?

Presidential Facts

Presidents, while very powerful people, are only human. They have certain likes and dislikes, as well as characteristics which make them unique. For instance, former President John F. Kennedy loved to sail in his boat and former President Ronald Reagan acted in movies before he took office.

Activity

Use the president books or an Internet search engine to match the characteristic with the president. Add that president's last name in the space provided.

1. He didn't like broccoli. **George** _____
2. He was so large that he needed a special bathtub. **William Howard** _____
3. He played football on the White House lawn. **Theodore** _____
4. He was the oldest man to be elected. **Ronald** _____
5. He didn't like to talk to dinner guests. **Calvin** _____
6. He had eleven brothers and sisters. **Benjamin** _____
7. He loved his black Scottie dog, Fala. **Franklin Delano** _____
8. He played the flute. **John Quincy** _____
9. He enjoyed playing golf. **Gerald** _____
10. He did not go to college. **Zachary** _____
11. He was an army general. **Dwight** _____
12. He became president after an assassination. **Lyndon** _____
13. He played the saxophone. **Bill** _____
14. He was the only president to serve two nonconsecutive terms. **Grover** _____
15. He died of pneumonia one month after his inauguration. **William Henry** _____
16. He once owned a men's clothing store. **Harry** _____
17. He was shot while watching a play at Ford's Theater. **Abraham** _____
18. His face appears on the one-dollar bill and the quarter. **George** _____
19. He was forced to resign his office. **Richard** _____
20. He helped run his family's peanut farm near Plains, Georgia. **Jimmy** _____

Word Bank

Bush	Adams	Clinton	Washington
Taft	Eisenhower	Roosevelt	Nixon
Reagan	Johnson	Cleveland	Harrison
Coolidge	Ford	Lincoln	Truman
Roosevelt	Taylor	Harrison	Carter

Extended Activities

☆ Which president never married? _____
☆ Which president held his wedding ceremony in the White House? _____
☆ Which president had 14 children? _____

Mount Rushmore

South Dakota's Black Hills are the backdrop for the impressive mountain sculpture, Mount Rushmore. The sculpture features the faces of four American presidents: (*from left to right*) George Washington, Thomas Jefferson, Theodore Roosevelt, and Abraham Lincoln.

Sculptor Gutzon Borglum began carving Mount Rushmore in 1927. He chose a site that rose 500 feet (152 m) above the neighboring mountains to create the 60-foot high faces. Drilling and blasting away the mountain took 14 years and cost one million dollars. It was difficult and dangerous work. Borglum died before finishing the monument in 1941, and his son, Lincoln, completed the project. In 1929, Congress made Mount Rushmore a national memorial. The National Park Service maintains it.

Activity

Use an encyclopedia or an Internet search engine to see a photo of Mount Rushmore. In the space below, write why you think each president was chosen to appear in the sculpture at Mount Rushmmore. Use your presidential books, encyclopedias, and the Internet to help formulate your answers.

1. **George Washington** _____

   _____

2. **Thomas Jefferson** _____

   _____

3. **Abraham Lincoln** _____

   _____

4. **Theodore Roosevelt** _____

   _____

Extended Activities

☆ Suppose there was space for another president to be carved into Mount Rushmore. Whom would you choose and why?

☆ Create a map from your city to Black Hills, South Dakota, or trace the route on a preprinted map.

Getting Personal with Presidents

Each president brings much that is unique to the White House. Some past presidents had children. Others had pets. Some loved to bowl and others loved to hunt. Different past presidents have belonged to different political parties, but almost all have one thing in common: the support of a vice president and a wife.

Activity

Select a president of your choice. Research his life using encyclopedias, books, and the Internet. Use the form below to record personal information.

Name _____

Middle Name _____

Born/Died _____

Birthplace _____

First Lady's Name _____

Children _____

Pets _____

Favorite Hobbies _____

Vice President _____

Political Party _____

Years Served _____

Other Jobs _____

George Washington:
The Father of His Country

George Washington was born February 22, 1732, in Westmoreland County, Virginia. He did not attend school regularly, but taught himself basic reading, writing, and math. His father died when he was eleven, leaving George to be raised by his brother, Lawrence.

George Washington married Martha Custis and adopted her two children, John and Martha. They lived at Mount Vernon, where he enjoyed farming, hunting, and fishing. Washington was the **commander** of the colonial army during the Revolutionary War. Because he was a great leader in the struggle for independence from Great Britain, Washington was the people's first choice to become president of the new nation.

In 1787, Washington **presided** over the Constitutional Convention, which drafted a **document** explaining the new system and its laws. He wanted the American democracy to have a strong central government. He also helped design the nation's capital city, which is named in his honor. Washington was a popular president who served two terms. However, he **declined** to run a third time.

George Washington died on December 14, 1799, from a throat infection. He is buried at Mount Vernon in the family **tomb**.

Activity

Using a dictionary, write definitions of the vocabulary words in bold type above on a separate sheet of paper. Then answer the questions below:

1. When and where was Washington born?_____

   _____

2. Name Washington's wife and adopted children. _____

   _____

3. What did he do before becoming president?_____

   _____

4. How did Washington help to create the new American government?_____

   _____

Extended Activities

☆ Describe a day in Washington's life as a farmer at Mount Vernon.

☆ Describe a day in Washington's life as an army general.

☆ Write a paragraph describing Washington's physical appearance.

☆ Research Mount Vernon in an encyclopedia, book, or on an Internet site.

☆ On a separate sheet of paper, write a description of the house and grounds at Mount Vernon.

Thomas Jefferson: Author of Our Liberty

Thomas Jefferson was born in a 1743 Virginia log cabin. His father was a farmer, who later became a justice of the peace, a **magistrate**, and a commander of the county **militia**. Thomas Jefferson was an excellent student. He also learned how to dance, play the violin, and ride horses.

He married Martha Wayles Skelton, a musician who played the **harpsichord** and the piano, on New Year's Day, 1772. Of their six children, only two daughters lived into adulthood. Martha's health was not good, and she died in 1782. Thomas Jefferson then focused his life on politics.

He was a philosopher, inventor, and architect. He was also an excellent writer who wrote many famous documents during the time that the United States was struggling for freedom from British rule. The most famous of these documents is The Declaration of Independence. It was officially adopted on July 4, 1776. Jefferson worked the rest of his life to uphold the **philosophy** he wrote about in the Declaration of Independence.

Thomas Jefferson died on July 4, 1826. He requested burial at his **estate**, called Monticello, and asked that a simple stone mark his gravesite. On it, he requested the following words: "Here was buried Thomas Jefferson, Author of the Declaration of American Independence, of the Statute of Virginia for religious freedom, & Father of the University of Virginia."

Activity

Using a dictionary, write definitions of the vocabulary words in bold type above on a separate sheet of paper. Then, answer the questions below:

1. When and where was Jefferson born? _____

_____

2. How many of Jefferson's six children survived into adulthood? _____

_____

3. What particular talents did Jefferson display? _____

_____

4. What is the most famous of Thomas Jefferson's written documents? _____

_____

Extended Activities

☆ Describe Jefferson's feelings on July 4, 1776, the day the Declaration of Independence was officially adopted.
☆ Explain why you think Jefferson chose the above words in particular for his gravestone.
☆ Write a paragraph describing Jefferson's physical appearance.
☆ Research the Jefferson Memorial in an encyclopedia, book, or on an Internet site. On a separate sheet of paper, write a description of the memorial.

Abraham Lincoln: The Great Emancipator

Abraham Lincoln was born February 12, 1809, in a log cabin in Kentucky.

Though he did not attend formal school very often, he enjoyed reading and became a self-taught prairie lawyer. Lincoln stood six feet four inches tall by age 21.

Abe, as he was nicknamed, married Mary Todd on November 4, 1842. They had four children: Robert, Edward, William, and Tad. Only Robert lived to adulthood.

Abraham Lincoln was elected 16th president of the United States in 1860. He fought against slavery, a common practice in the Southern states. Because of this, the Southern states **seceded** to form a new country. The Civil War began on April 12, 1861. Lincoln hated war and wanted the states to come together again. He made many speeches against slavery, and, in 1863, wrote the **Emancipation Proclamation**, which demanded the freedom of slaves. However, his words did not stop the fighting. In November 1863, Lincoln delivered his most famous speech, the Gettysburg **Address**, while dedicating a battlefield cemetery. Next, he encouraged Congress to pass the 13th **amendment**, which said that slavery could not exist in the United States. The amendment became law in 1865, after the war had ended.

Abraham Lincoln was **assassinated** on April 14, 1865, while watching a play at Ford's Theater in Washington, D.C. He was shot in the back of the head by John Wilkes Booth and died the next morning. He is buried in Springfield, Illinois.

Activity

Using a dictionary or history reference, write definitions of the vocabulary words in bold type above on a separate sheet of paper. Then answer the questions below:

1. When and where was Lincoln born? _____

  _____

2. Name Lincoln's wife and children. _____

  _____

3. How did Lincoln feel about slavery? _____

  _____

4. When and where was he assassinated? _____

  _____

Extended Activities

☆ Write a list of ten questions you would like to ask President Lincoln.

☆ Read the Gettysburg Address to your class.

☆ Make an illustrated time line showing six events in Lincoln's life.

☆ Research the Lincoln Memorial in an encyclopedia, book, or on an Internet site. On a separate sheet of paper, write a description of the memorial.

Franklin Delano Roosevelt: Provider of a New Deal

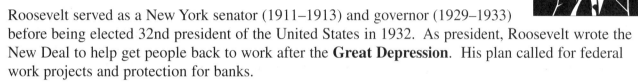

Franklin Delano Roosevelt was born January 30, 1882, in Hyde Park, New York. His father was the founder of **Consolidated** Coal Company and the director of the Delaware and Hudson Railroad. Franklin attended a private grammar school where he became interested in politics. He became a practicing attorney in 1907.

He married Eleanor in 1905. They had five children: Franklin Jr., Anna, James, Elliott, and John. Franklin Roosevelt was stricken with polio, a crippling disease, in 1921. He was unable to stand without the help of leg **braces**.

Roosevelt served as a New York senator (1911–1913) and governor (1929–1933) before being elected 32nd president of the United States in 1932. As president, Roosevelt wrote the New Deal to help get people back to work after the **Great Depression**. His plan called for federal work projects and protection for banks.

As the only man to be elected to the presidency four terms, he led the country during the attack on Pearl Harbor and World War II. Under his direction, millions of men and women served in the armed forces until the defeat of Germany and Japan in 1945.

Franklin Delano Roosevelt died of a **cerebral hemorrhage** while on vacation in Warm Springs, Georgia, on April 12, 1945. He is buried in Hyde Park, New York.

═══ Activity ═══

Using a dictionary or history reference book, write definitions of the vocabulary words in bold type above on a separate sheet of paper. Then answer the following questions:

1. When and where was Roosevelt born? _____

   _____

2. Name Roosevelt's wife and children. _____

   _____

3. What was the purpose of the New Deal? _____

   _____

4. Explain why Roosevelt was unable to stand or walk without help. _____

   _____

═══ Extended Activities ═══

☆ How did Roosevelt use "fireside chats" to encourage the American people?

☆ Make a list of nine New Deal projects. Explain what each one did.

☆ Explain the events of December 7, 1941, which was "A day which will live in infamy," according to President Roosevelt.

☆ Research the Roosevelt Memorial in an encyclopedia, book, or on an Internet site. On a separate sheet of paper, write a description of the memorial.

Presidential Patriots

Many presidents have been elected because of their service to our country. They worked as governors, congressmen, diplomats, or military leaders before serving as the leader of our country.

Activity

Research the lives of the presidents below. Make an **X** in each column that applies, showing which men held which positions. Use *Eyewitness: Presidents* or other reference books to help you complete this chart.

Each president will have a check in at least two different columns.

#	Presidents	Diplomat	Military Leader	Governor	Congress	Vice President
2	John Adams					
3	Thomas Jefferson					
8	Martin Van Buren					
13	Millard Fillmore					
26	Theodore Roosevelt					
28	Woodrow Wilson					
30	Calvin Coolidge					
33	Harry Truman					
34	Dwight Eisenhower					
35	John Kennedy					
37	Richard Nixon					
39	Jimmy Carter					

Uncle Sam and Old Glory

by Delno C. West and Jean M. West

This book examines the stories behind fifteen important American symbols. Whether studying objects, animals, or characters, your students will enjoy learning why we value the symbols and how they represent the United States to the rest of the world.

Sample Plan

Lesson I

- Add entries for symbols to the wall chart of descriptive words.
- Read "The Liberty Bell" (page 16) and "The Statue of Liberty" (page 19).
- Assign "Lady Liberty" (page 22 of this book).
- Read "The Great Seal of the United States" (page 12) and "The American Bald Eagle" (page 15).
- Assign "The Great Seal" (page 23 of this book).
- Assign "Bald Eagle" (page 55 of this book). Ask students to create illustrated symbol reports.

Lesson II

- Read "Uncle Sam" (page 20).
- Assign "Uncle Sam Wilson" (page 24 of this book).
- Read "The American Flag" (page 11).
- Assign "Flag Etiquette" (page 20) and "Flag Gallery and History" (page 61 of this book).
- Begin planning a flag ceremony (page 73 of this book).
- Distribute and memorize the Pledge of Allegiance (page 21 of this book).

Lesson III

- Read "The Mayflower" (page 24) and "The Pilgrim" (page 27).
- Assign "Journey to America" (page 25 of this book).
- Complete "Packing for the Voyage" (page 44 of this book).

Lesson IV

- Read "The Log Cabin" (page 32), "The Buffalo" (page 35), and "The Cowboy" (page 36).
- Assign "Buffalo" (page 56 of this book).
- Assign "The Log Cabin" (page 28 of this book).
- Assign "Cowboy Days" (page 29 of this book).

Lesson V

- Make an all American time capsule (page 72 of this book).
- Finish planning the flag ceremony (page 73 of this book) and an all American picnic (page 71 of this book).
- Play games (page 72 of this book).
- Complete "Create a Symbol" (page 27 of this book).
- Share individual reports on patriotic symbols.

Overview of Activities

Setting the Stage

1. Be sure your students understand that a symbol is an object used to represent something abstract (e.g., a peace dove). Ask your students to think of five concrete items that are symbols of their community, school, or personal lives. Complete a "Daily Writing Topic" on page 47 about personal symbols.

2. Begin a list of characteristics that are true of most American symbols, like courage, strength, and honor. Discuss how such ideas help to define the American spirit.

Enjoying the Book

1. Make a chart categorizing the symbols in *Uncle Sam and Old Glory* into characters, animals, or objects. Brainstorm an additional list of American symbols and categorize them. Ask students to support their selections with characteristics, if necessary.

2. Ask students to create individual symbol reports to be completed with the help of reference materials or the Web sites listed in the bibliography during the study of this book. They may make drawings or create models from art materials.

3. Read "The Liberty Bell" on page 16. The page suggests three freedoms that are guarded by the Liberty Bell. Have students write a summary of our basic freedoms (found in the Bill of Rights) and a statement to explain the impact of each on their personal lives. Share *A Kids' Guide to the Bill of Rights: Curfews, Censorship, and the 100-Pound Giant* by Kathleen Krull (Avon Books, 1999). Read "The Statue of Liberty" on page 19. Discuss the meaning of the statue's inscription for immigrants and assign "Lady Liberty" on page 22 of this book. Search the Internet for photos of the memorial.

4. Read "The Great Seal of the United States" on page 12. Introduce students to the meaning of the individual items on the seal and assign page 23 of this book. Look for the seal on a collection of common items (paper money, etc.). Read "The American Bald Eagle" on page 15. Encourage students to explore the problems caused to bald eagles by loss of habitat and pesticides. Ask them to complete page 55 of this book.

5. Read "The American Flag" on page 11 and complete "Flag Etiquette" on page 20 of this book. Read additional nonfiction information in *The Flag We Love* by Pam Munoz Ryan (Charlesbridge Books, 2001). Discuss the flag ceremony on page 73 of this book and practice reciting the Pledge of Allegiance on page 21. Distribute "Flag Gallery and History" on page 61 of this book.

6. Read "The Mayflower" on page 24 and "The Pilgrim" on page 27 of the book. Assign "Journey to America," on page 25 of this book for additional information about the ship, then have students help the Pilgrims decide what to take along in "Packing for the Voyage" on page 44 of this book. Be sure your students understand the hardships and dangers endured by Pilgrims in order to live in a free country. Consider the rules that were necessary to guide the new colony. Complete "The First Thanksgiving," on page 26 of this book.

7. Read "Yankee Doodle" on page 23 of the book and explore the history of log cabins on page 28 of this book. Read "The Buffalo" on page 35 and learn about the digestive system of ruminant animals on page 56 of this book. Display examples of each type of vegetation eaten by bison: grass, forb, and browse.

18

Overview of Activities *(cont.)*

8. Read "The Cowboy" on page 36. Discuss life on a cattle ranch and the lonely job of a cowboy, emphasizing their courage and strength working in difficult conditions. List their duties and show pictures of their clothing and equipment. Distribute "Cowboy Days" on page 29 of this book. Compare/contrast the life of a frontier cowboy with a contemporary one. Look for examples of cowboy culture (songs, poetry, etc.) in the library and on the Internet to share with the class.

Extending the Book

1. Ask the music teacher at your school to help students learn several patriotic songs. Everyone should memorize "The Star-Spangled Banner" on page 70 of this book for the Flag Ceremony. Finish planning the ceremony and have a rehearsal. Determine a time at the beginning of the day when all students can gather outdoors for a flag raising, the Pledge of Allegiance, and the national anthem. Students may reassemble to lower the flag before leaving for the day.

2. Discuss what symbols of America should be included in the all American time capsule on page 72 of this book. Refine the list and begin collecting the items to fill a container. Allow students to agree on a safe place to store the finished capsule.

3. Students working in pairs should use their imaginations to create a new patriotic symbol, as described on page 27 of this book. They should provide a colored drawing or model as well as a written explanation of the meaning and colors. If possible, display the new symbols in the school library.

Flag Etiquette

The United States flag has seven red and six white stripes, which represent the original thirteen colonies. There is a star for each of the fifty states on the blue rectangle called the union. The Federal Flag Code is a set of rules for displaying the flag. Here are some of the rules:

☆ The flag should never be displayed with the union down, except as a signal of distress or danger to life or property.

☆ The flag should never touch the ground or water.

☆ The flag should never be displayed or stored in a way that it could be torn, soiled, or damaged.

☆ The flag, when it is in such condition that it can no longer be displayed, should be destroyed in a dignified way, usually by burning.

☆ When the national anthem is played and the flag is displayed, all people should face the flag and salute or cover their hearts.

☆ No other flag should be placed above the flag of the United States of America. If both flags are on the same level, the American flag should appear on the left side.

☆ The flag of the United States of America should fly at the center and at the highest point when grouped with a number of other flags on staffs.

☆ When displayed either horizontally or vertically against a wall, the union should be on the observer's left.

Activity

Read the sentences and fill in the blanks.

1. The flag should never touch the ___ ___ (o) ___ ___ ___ .
2. No other f ___ a ( ) should ever be displayed above the U. S. flag.
3. When displayed ___ ___ ___ ___ ___ ___ ___ (l) ___ y, the union should be on the upper left.
4. The flag should never be t ( ) ___ n or soiled.
5. A flag in poor condition should be ___ ___ ___ ___ (r) ___ ( ) ___ (d) by burning.
6. The ___ (l) ___ ___ should never be hung with the union down except to show danger.

Arrange the circled letters to spell another name for the flag.

___ ___ ___   ___ ___ ___ ___ ___

Extended Activity

☆ Here is a list of important days on which to display the flag. Mark these dates on your family's calendar and proudly display your American flag!

Inauguration Day (January 20)
Presidents' Day (third Monday in February)
Armed Forces Day (third Sunday in May)
Memorial Day (May 30, officially observed the last Monday in May)

Flag Day (June 14)
Independence Day (July 4)
Veterans Day (November 11)

The Pledge

Francis Bellamy, a magazine publisher, wrote the first Pledge of Allegiance for school children to recite in celebration of Columbus Day, October 12, 1892. It was published in *The Youth's Companion*, a popular family magazine of the day. The original pledge read as follows:

> "I pledge allegiance to my Flag and to the Republic for which it stands, one nation, indivisible, with liberty and justice for all."

Some changes have been made to the original. The first National Flag Conference in Washington, D.C., on June 14, 1923, added "the Flag of the United States of America" in place of "my Flag." Congress officially recognized the Pledge of Allegiance in 1942, but one year later, the Supreme Court ruled that school children could not be forced to recite it. In June 1954, the words "under God" were added. Today, about half of our fifty states observe laws that encourage the recitation of the Pledge of Allegiance in the classroom.

Activity

Number the phrases to show the correct order in which to recite the Pledge of Allegiance.

_____ I pledge allegiance	
_____ and to the Republic for which it stands	
_____ one nation	
_____ to the Flag	
_____ of the United States of America	
_____ indivisible	
_____ under God	
_____ with liberty and justice for all	

Lady Liberty

Located in New York Harbor, the Statue of Liberty was a gift of friendship from the people of France to the people of the United States. It is a national monument and a symbol of freedom in America. The Statue of Liberty was dedicated on October 28, 1886. It was restored and repaired in 1986.

Ellis Island is part of the Statue of Liberty National Monument. Between 1892 and 1954, approximately 12 million immigrants entering the United States through the port of New York were received at Ellis Island. The main building is a museum dedicated to the history of immigration.

Emma Lazarus (1849–1887) wrote this inscription on the statue's tablet. It greets people entering this country.

> "Give me your tired, your poor, Your huddled masses yearning to breathe free, The wretched refuse of your teeming shore. Send these, the homeless, tempest-tost to me, I lift my lamp beside the golden door!"

These dimensions will help you better understand the size of the statue.

Head from chin to top:	17' 3"	(5.26 m)	Size of fingernail:	13" x 10"	(33 x 25.4 cm)
Head from ear to ear:	10' 0"	(3.05 m)	Right arm length:	42' 0"	(12.80 m)
Each eye:	2' 6"	(.76 m)	Length of foot:	25'	(7.62 m)
Length of nose:	4' 6"	(1.48 m)	Tablet, length:	23' 7"	(7.19 m)
Width of mouth:	3' 0"	(.91 m)	Tablet, width:	13' 7"	(4.14 m)
Length of hand:	16' 5"	(5.00 m)	Heel to top of head:	111' 1"	(33.86 m)
Index finger:	8' 0"	(2.44 m)			

Activity

Measure the heel-to-top-of-head dimension and draw the Statue of Liberty on the playground to show its total height.

Extended Activities

☆ Memorize the inscription from the Statue of Liberty's tablet and explain what it means to immigrants.

☆ In your journal, write a short story describing what it would be like to come to America for the first time.

☆ Do research and write a report explaining the importance of Ellis Island. Include historic information about immigration.

☆ Use an encyclopedia or the Internet to do further research on the Statue of Liberty. Write down five new facts that you learned.

The Great Seal

The founding fathers believed the new, independent nation needed an emblem—something that would stand as a symbol of the United States. On July 4, 1776, Benjamin Franklin, John Adams, and Thomas Jefferson were asked to create a seal for the United States of America. The final design for the Great Seal was approved on June 20, 1782.

The Great Seal shows a beautiful and powerful bird—the eagle—facing front, with its wings spread. On its chest is a shield with thirteen red and white stripes, one for each of the original colonies. In its talons, the eagle holds an olive branch, which symbolizes peace. It also holds a bundle of thirteen arrows, which are symbols of war. In its beak, it carries a scroll with the words, "E Pluribus Unum" which is Latin for "out of many, one." There are 13 stars in a blue field above the eagle's head. They symbolize the addition of the United States into the other free nations of the world.

Activity

Explain the significance of these symbols on the Great Seal:

1. eagle _____

   _____

2. arrows _____

   _____

3. olive branch _____

   _____

4. red and white stripes _____

   _____

5. shield _____

   _____

6. thirteen _____

   _____

7. stars _____

   _____

8. What does the phrase, "out of many, one," mean to Americans? _____

   _____

Extended Activity

☆ Using an encyclopedia, book, or the Internet, find out which bird Benjamin Franklin felt to be a better symbol of the United States. Then write a paragraph arguing for or against his preference.

Uncle Sam Wilson

Samuel Wilson (1766–1854) was a soldier in the Revolutionary War. In 1789, he moved to Troy, New York, where he worked as a meat packer. It was there that Wilson earned the nickname "Uncle Sam."

During the War of 1812, Wilson provided pork and beef to the Army in barrels labeled "U.S." The letters "U.S." did not represent the United States in those days. When a Federal inspector asked a worker the meaning of the letters on the meat barrels, the man said, "Uncle Sam." He meant Uncle Sam Wilson, his employer.

Uncle Sam became an American symbol. He is depicted as a tall, thin man with a white beard. He is typically dressed in a blue jacket with tails, red bow tie, white shirt, and red and white striped pants. His top hat is blue with a red and white striped brim. There are white stars on his hat and the lapels of his jacket. The most famous picture of Uncle Sam appeared on an Army recruiting poster used in World Wars I and II. The poster reads, "I Want You for the U.S. Army."

Activity

Think of a current national event or problem. In the space below, draw a political cartoon or poster including the image of Uncle Sam. Add a title on the line. Color your picture with colored pencils or markers.

Title

Extended Activities

☆ Use the Internet to look for information about Troy, New York. What does this city do to honor "Uncle Sam" Wilson?

☆ Collect items that have the image of Uncle Sam for a classroom display.

Journey to America

Seventy men and women and thirty two children sailed for America in September 1620 on a small ship called the *Mayflower*. Their trip across the Atlantic Ocean was a difficult one, complicated by wild storms. Sometimes it seemed that the ship would break apart. Two men died and one baby was born during the 65-day voyage. The Pilgrims had been granted land in the Virginia territory, but their ship went off course. They made their first settlement near Plymouth, Massachusetts.

Activity

Pretend you are a reporter at a news conference on the day the *Mayflower* Pilgrims reached shore. Write three questions you would like to ask them.

1. _____

2. _____

3. _____

In 1955, a group of British people had an idea to construct a replica of the original Pilgrim ship to honor the cooperation between America and England. They built a full-sized model and called it *Mayflower II*. The new ship was exactly like the original. On April 20, 1957, a crew of 34 men began the voyage across the Atlantic Ocean using no modern equipment. They arrived at Plymouth Rock on June 13. Today, the *Mayflower II* is anchored on the waterfront at Plymouth, Massachusetts.

What would you want to see first if you visited the *Mayflower II?* _____

_____

Why is the *Mayflower* important to our history? _____

_____

Why did the English build and sail the *Mayflower II?* _____

_____

Extended Activities

☆ To show the size of the *Mayflower*, mark a 90' x 26' (27 m x 8 m) space on the school playground with chalk. Stand 102 student "passengers" inside the lines.

☆ Make a cross-section drawing of the inside of the *Mayflower*. Label supplies, people, and living quarters.

The First Thanksgiving

Some people, called Pilgrims, came to America in search of religious freedom. Others, called Strangers, came to find wealth in a new land. They knew they would all have to live and work together, so they agreed on a basic plan of government called the Mayflower Compact. The first winter in the colony was very difficult. Many people got sick. Some even died. When spring arrived, the Pilgrims became friends with a Native American named Squanto who taught them how to plant crops and catch fish. By fall, they had enough food to celebrate the first Thanksgiving.

Activity

Write three laws that might have been part of the Mayflower Compact, which helped everyone get along.

1. _____

   _____

2. _____

   _____

3. _____

   _____

Make a list of foods that might have been served at the first Thanksgiving.

1. _____
2. _____
3. _____
4. _____
5. _____
6. _____

Extended Activity

☆ Using a Venn diagram, show how the first Thanksgiving was different from our celebrations today.

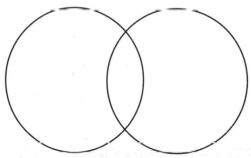

26

Create a Symbol

National symbols express our ideas and feelings about the American way of life. As you have learned, they may relate to historic events or to our beliefs in freedom, equality and democracy. Some contemporary symbols include the peace sign and colored ribbons worn to indicate support for different causes.

Activity

Think about the symbols in this unit. Then use this form to design and describe a new symbol based on your ideas. You may want to work in pairs to complete this assignment.

Symbol _____

Story _____

_____

_____

Description _____

_____

_____

The Log Cabin

Log cabins were houses made entirely of logs. Swedish colonists introduced this type of house to America in 1638. By the time of the American Revolution, log cabins had become the typical dwelling of people who lived on the frontier. Three American presidents were born in log cabins: William Henry Harrison, Abraham Lincoln, and Ulysses S. Grant.

William H.
Harrison

Abraham
Lincoln

Ulysses
S. Grant

Log cabins were popular among pioneers because they could be built by just one person with an axe and a hunting knife. The builder filled in the cracks between the logs with moss and mud to keep out the wind and cold. Log cabins seldom had windowpanes, as glass wasn't readily available. Instead, people hung greased paper in the window-frames. The floor of a log cabin was made of either hard-packed dirt or of the flat side of logs that had been split in half.

Sometimes log-cabin building was a community activity. Neighbors would gather to build a cabin together. Many times they would have parties with food and dancing while they built a new dwelling.

When pioneers reached the Great Plains, they found very few trees. These people had to make houses out of sod instead. But farther west, in the wooded Rocky Mountains, log cabins began to appear once more!

Activity

In the space below, design your own log cabin. Draw a picture of the both the outside and the inside of the cabin. How many rooms would your cabin have? Label the rooms (bedroom, kitchen, etc.), and then color your picture.

Extended Activity

☆ Use an encyclopedia or the Internet to see photos of a real log cabin. Write down five details you observed.

Cowboy Days

A cowboy's life was full of danger and hard work. His main job was to take care of cattle, which might mean freeing them from a barbed wire fence, nursing them through sickness, or helping them give birth. Cowboys had time to repair their equipment or mend fences when the cattle grazed on the range. Small groups of cowboys went on roundups and trail drives that took them far away from the nearest towns for several days or weeks at a time. Often, they would be injured in roping accidents or falls, or trampled by herds of stampeding cattle.

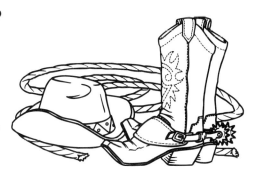

On a ranch, groups of cowboys lived together in bunkhouses. They worked from dawn to dusk and were only able to go to town on their days off. Cowboys wore wide brimmed hats to protect their eyes from the sun and neck scarves to keep dust out of their mouths, noses, and ears. They wore vests over their shirts to hold small personal items and leather leg coverings called chaps, to protect their pants from being torn by thorns and other rough objects. Knee-high boots and spurs helped the cowboy control his horse.

On trail drives, cowboys ate a hearty breakfast of bacon, griddle cakes, eggs, ham, sausage, steak, cornbread, biscuits, and black coffee. At the end of the day, they had a dinner of beans, bacon, and biscuits after the cattle were settled for the night. Cowboys often had to sleep on the ground near their horses. Hard working cowboys helped make the West a productive region of the United States. They came to symbolize courage, independence, and the frontier spirit.

Activity

What do you think would be best thing and worst thing about being a cowboy?

Best: _____

Worst: _____

Imagine you are a cowboy on a trail drive. List five of your daily activities.

1. _____

2. _____

3. _____

4. _____

5. _____

Extended Activity

On a separate sheet of paper, list five modern inventions that make the life of a cowboy easier and/or safer than it was in the frontier days.

A is for America

by Devin Scillian

This alphabet book presents American history, geography, and culture. Each letter offers a two-page illustration, a four-line rhyming stanza, and a brief entry with nonfiction information.

Sample Plan

Lesson I

- Continue adding to the wall chart of descriptive words.

- Show the book, pointing out the letter-specific details in the illustrations.

- Encourage independent reading of the *Discover America State by State* series alphabet books by Sleeping Bear Press.

Lesson II

- Read A–F.

- Complete "Crazy Stories" (page 46).

- Read G–M.

- Complete "Immigration" (page 34).

- Use the entire tbook to complete "Timely Dates" (page 35).

Lesson III

- Read N–S

- Complete "Patriots and Patriotism" (page 38).

- Use the entire book to complete "Latitude and Longitude" (page 36).

- Complete "Nifty Fifty" (page 51).

- Write an ode to America on page 48.

Lesson IV

- Read T–Z.

- Complete "Veterans' Day" (page 65) and "A New Reason to Celebrate" (page 39).

- Complete the national parks locator map (page 63).

- Complete an American poem (page 37).

- Assign "All Around Town" (page 66).

Lesson V

- Compile all American ABCs (page 33).

- Design commemorative postage stamps (page 40).

- Share an all American picnic (page 71).

- Read about Norman Rockwell (page 67) and paint a mural (page 69).

- Share the individual state alphabet books with younger classes.

Overview of Activities

Setting the Stage

1. Brainstorm an ABC list of words which relate to America. Explain the format of *A is for America* and discuss a few pages of illustration.

2. Display a large "People, Places, and Things" chart and explain that you will be listing words from the book in each category. Be sure that students search the illustrations for vocabulary not present in the text.

3. Have a collection of individual state alphabet books from Sleeping Bear Press for students to read independently.

4. Prepare an interactive map bulletin board, located on page 74 of this book, to locate state capitals and cities named throughout the textbook.

Enjoying the Book

1. Ask students to read aloud the rhyming stanzas and the brief text (A–F) and continue adding to the wall chart of descriptive words. Your list should contain adjectives like "highest, largest, better, slender."

2. Use the map bulletin board to locate cities as they are mentioned (B—Boston, C—Chicago, etc.). You may extend this activity with an atlas or Internet search of other American cities that begin with a specific letter.

3. Demonstrate the parts of speech in "Crazy Stories" on page 46 of this book. You may reuse this activity at any time during the study of this book.

4. Read G–M and continue adding to the wall chart of descriptive words. Focus on the "I" page and ask students what they know about their heritage. Complete "Immigration" on page 34 of this book as a homework assignment. Discuss evidence of other cultures in American life (e.g., pizza, soccer, and piñatas) and explain the importance of Ellis Island and the Statue of Liberty to immigrants.

5. Use information from the entire book to complete "Timely Dates" on page 35.

6. Write a poem of tribute called an ode to America. You will find an example on page 48 of this book. Students will need lists of rhyming words to complete this assignment, which may be completed in small groups.

7. Read N–S. Discuss the idea of patriotism. Ask how the concept may change from day to day depending on current events, and ask what individuals (particularly children) can do to show their patriotism. Complete "Patriots and Patriotism" on page 38 of this book.

8. Complete "Latitude and Longitude" on page 36 of this book, using information from the entire book, as well as research materials. Review the terms *latitude* and *longitude*, so that after determining the correct states, students can add the map locations.

Overview of Activities *(cont.)*

=== **Enjoying the Book** *(cont.)* ===

9. Ask students to complete "Nifty Fifty" on page 51 in this book while working in cooperative groups. (You may need to provide calendars for the assignment.) Students will read admittance dates for each state and organize numbers 1–50. Post the work of the first group to finish correctly.

10. Read T–Z. Complete "Veterans' Day" on page 65 and "A New Reason to Celebrate" on page 39 of this book. Design and display a collection of greeting cards for the new holidays.

11. For more map practice, complete the national parks locator map on page 63 of this book.

12. Assign each student a different letter to use when completing the American poem on page 37. Combine the best poems in a class book.

=== **Extending the Book** ===

1. Have students work in groups to compile personal lists of all American ABCs on page 33. They may use the lists to create original ABC books about America to share with younger students. You may make an enlargement of the map on page 74 to use as a book cover.

2. Design commemorative postage stamps on page 40 of this book.

3. Read about Norman Rockwell on page 67 and paint a mural as described on page 69 of this book.

4. Complete "All Around Town" on page 66 of this book, compiling a list of public buildings and landmarks that have a patriotic connection.

5. Share an all American picnic, described on page 71 of this book, with another class. Assign students to bring hot dogs, condiments, popcorn, paper plates, small paper bags, apple pies, napkins, and plastic forks.

All American ABCs

Use this page to brainstorm alphabetical lists in one of these categories:

☆ states and city names

☆ American inventors and inventions

☆ national parks, landmarks, memorials, and monuments

☆ natural resources and manufactured goods

☆ nouns that have special meaning in your state

A _____

B _____

C _____

D _____

E _____

F _____

G _____

H _____

I _____

J _____

K _____

L _____

M _____

N _____

O _____

P _____

Q _____

R _____

S _____

T _____

U _____

V _____

W _____

X _____

Y _____

Z _____

Immigration

Most early settlers came to America because they wanted to begin a new life in a free country. In their old countries, some people were poor, living under the strict rule of a king, queen, or other authority figure. They left almost all of their possessions behind to start a new life. The Statue of Liberty greeted these settlers in New York Harbor.

Activity

What do you know about your heritage? Here are some questions to ask adult members of your family:

1. What were your parents' and grandparents' names?

   _____

   _____

2. Where and when were they born?

   _____

   _____

3. Why and from where did your family immigrate to the United States?

   _____

   _____

4. When and how did they arrive?

   _____

   _____

Print out a copy of the United States map on page 74. Color the states in which members of your family live or have lived.

Extended Activities

☆ Learn more about America's immigrants. Ask the above questions of a neighbor or family friend.

☆ Tally the number of states in which each student's family lives or has lived. Write these numbers on a copy of the map on page 74.

Timely Dates

The history of any country is marked by important events such as when it was founded, which individuals have made a difference by their words and actions, and what discoveries and conflicts have occurred.

Activity

Use information from the book to add the dates of the events below.

1. The Liberty Bell was rung to announce the reading of the Declaration of Independence. _____

2. The Liberty Bell cracked. _____

3. Orville and Wilbur Wright flew the first airplane at Kitty Hawk. _____

4. The Constitution was written. _____

5. Lincoln issued the Emancipation Proclamation. _____

6. The birthday of Martin Luther King, Jr. was made a national holiday. _____.

7. Neil Armstrong walked on the moon. _____

8. There was a gunfight at the OK Corral. _____

9. Whitcomb Judson invented the zipper. _____

10. Zip codes were added to mailing addresses. _____

Use reference books to add these dates for events from the book.

11. Civil rights activist Rosa Parks was arrested for refusing to sit at the back of the bus. _____

12. The 19th Amendment was passed, granting women the right to vote. _____

13. Uncle Tom's Cabin, a novel about slavery, was published. _____

14. Gold was discovered at Sutter's Mill, California. _____

15. Congress made "The Star Spangled Banner" our national anthem. _____

Extended Activity

☆ Work with a friend to put all the dates in sequential order, then record them on a time line and add illustrations.

Latitude and Longitude

Latitude and longitude refer to a system of geometrical coordinates that are used to define the location of a particular place on Earth. Latitude gives the location of places north or south of the equator. It is shown by angular measurements from 0° at the equator to 90° at the north and south poles. Longitude shows the location of a place east or west of the prime meridian. It is measured in angles ranging from 0° at the prime meridian to 180° at the international date line.

Activity

Add the states in which each city can be found. Then use a map to add latitude and longitude coordinates.

CITY	STATE	LATITUDE	LONGITUDE
1. Philadelphia	_____	_____	_____
2. Boston	_____	_____	_____
3. Chicago	_____	_____	_____
4. Cleveland	_____	_____	_____
5. Charlotte	_____	_____	_____
6. Cincinnati	_____	_____	_____
7. New Orleans	_____	_____	_____
8. New York City	_____	_____	_____
9. Wheeling	_____	_____	_____
10. Dover	_____	_____	_____
11. Detroit	_____	_____	_____
12. Phoenix	_____	_____	_____
13. Tombstone	_____	_____	_____
14. Jamestown	_____	_____	_____
15. Dallas	_____	_____	_____

Extended Activity

☆ Find the latitude and longitude of your city, as well as the cities in which your parents were born.

American Poem

American poets have long written poems in celebration of the cities and landscapes they love. Walt Whitman (1819–1892) wrote a famous poem called "I Hear America Singing." Robert Frost (1874–1963) wrote about the New England states in poems such as "Stopping by Woods on a Snowy Evening." Maya Angelou (1928–) read her poem, "On the Pulse of Morning," in celebration of the United States during the presidential inauguration of Bill Clinton in 1993.

Activity

In the space below, write ten things that you like best about your country, state, city, or neighborhood. Then write a poem incorporating as many of these details as possible.

1. _____   6. _____
2. _____   7. _____
3. _____   8. _____
4. _____   9. _____
5. _____   10. _____

_____
Title

_____
_____
_____
_____
_____
_____

Extended Activity

In an encyclopedia or the Internet, find one of the poems mentioned above. In a paragraph, explain what you think the poet likes best about America.

Patriots and Patriotism

Patriotism refers to the love for one's country and the belief in that country's ideals and goals. Some famous American patriots include reformer Susan B. Anthony, educator Booker T. Washington, and labor leader Cesar Chavez. All United States presidents are considered patriots.

Activity

Choose a patriot from the list below or choose another patriot with your teacher's approval. Using an encyclopedia, book, or the Internet, gather together biographical information and answer the following questions.

Patriot List

Susan B. Anthony	Jane Addams	Ziolkowski	Eleanor Roosevelt
Booker T. Washington	Gutzon Borglum	Martin Luther King, Jr.	Richard Feynman
Cesar Chavez	Harriet Tubman	Chief Joseph	Rosa Parks
	Korczak		

What is this patriot's name? _____

When was this patriot born?_____

What was this patriot's main job? _____

List three things that this patriot did to help America and its inhabitants. _____

_____

_____

_____

Extended Activity

☆ List five actions you could take to demonstrate your patriotism. Choose one or more and complete them!

1. _____
2. _____
3. _____
4. _____
5. _____

A New Reason to Celebrate

There are many uniquely American holidays. Some, like the Fourth of July, celebrate events of historical significance. Others honor the contributions of famous people such as George Washington, Abraham Lincoln, and Dr. Martin Luther King, Jr.

Activity

Pretend you are part of a committee organized to plan a new all American holiday. Use the form below to explain your new holiday.

Name of holiday: _____

Date: _____

Person or event to honor: _____

Reason for the selection:_____

List three things you and your friends will do to celebrate.

1. _____

2. _____

3. _____

Extended Activity

Choose one of the holidays below. Locate its date on a calendar and explain its historical background.

Labor Day   **Memorial Day**   **Presidents' Day**
Independence Day   **Martin Luther King, Jr. Day**   **Thanksgiving Day**

Name of holiday: _____

Date: _____

Person or event to honor: _____

Reason for the selection: _____

List three things people do to celebrate this holiday.

1. _____

2. _____

3. _____

A is for America

Commemorative Postage Stamps

Each year, the United States Postal Service issues stamps to honor specific people, places, or events in American history. These are called commemorative stamps. Stamps may only depict persons who are no longer living or an event that is more than fifty years old. The first American commemorative stamps, issued in 1876, honored the first hundred years of postal service in the United States. They were three-cent stamps.

Commemorative stamps are typically very colorful. They are issued in sheets instead of rolls. You can buy them from your local post office.

Activity

Choose a person, place, or thing from *A is for America* and design a commemorative stamp to honor your selection. Don't forget to add the current cost of postage.

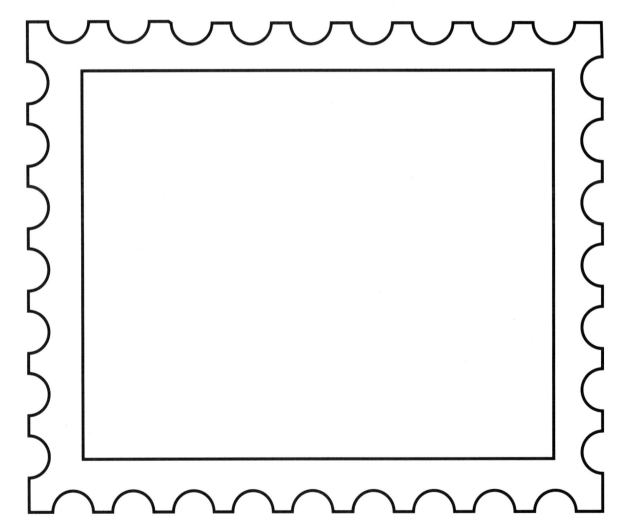

Explain why you chose this topic to commemorate. _____

_____

A Day in the Life of the President

Requirements

The Constitution states that the president of the United States must be a natural-born American citizen, at least 35 years old. He or she must have lived in the United States at least fourteen years before inauguration. A president may serve no more than two consecutive four-year terms. If a president commits a serious crime, he or she may be impeached (removed from office) by a two-thirds vote of the House of Representatives.

Duties

The president is commander-in-chief of all the armed forces. He or she may direct troops to movement on land and sea in time of war or peace. It is the president's job to protect the American citizens and take actions to defend the Constitution. The president leads the government, which enforces our laws. He or she has the power to sign or veto bills and laws presented by Congress. (*Veto* means "reject.") The president's Cabinet, or group of advisors, helps him or her make decisions. With Senate approval, the president appoints members of the Supreme Court and other important government officials. The president also meets with and entertains visiting foreign dignitaries and ambassadors. He or she may discuss foreign policy, negotiate trade agreements, and host formal dinners. In addition, each year the president performs ceremonial duties such as giving medals to heroes, greeting visitors, and lighting the White House Christmas tree.

Oath

The president takes the oath of office at noon on January 20th of the year following the election. Here is the official oath:

> "I do solemnly swear (or affirm) that I will faithfully execute the office of President of the United States, and will to the best of my ability, preserve, protect, and defend the Constitution of the United States."

Activity

What is the most important duty of the president? Explain your answer. _____

_____

How could the way the president does his or her job affect you and your family?_____

_____

Make a list of things you can do now to prepare yourself to be president. _____

_____

_____

Extended Activities

☆ Design a postage stamp showing the president performing one of his or her duties.

☆ Design a chart showing the names and positions of all current cabinet members.

Presidential Epitaphs

An epitaph is an inscription on a tomb or gravestone commemorating the one who is buried there. Often an epitaph will mention something significant that the deceased person accomplished in his or her lifetime. For instance, Thomas Jefferson requested his epitaph state that he wrote the Declaration of Independence and was the father of the University of Virginia.

Activity

Below, you will find epitaphs that could appear on the tombstones of some of our presidents. Use encyclopedias, books, and the Internet to help you fill in the name of the president each epitaph describes, as well as the year he died.

1. Here lies _____, the author of the Declaration of Independence.
   (1743–_____)

2. Here lies "Old Hickory,"_____. Remember the Alamo.
   (1767–_____)

3. Here lies _____. He served only one month in office.
   (1773–_____)

4. Here lies "Old Rough and Ready," _____.
   (1784–_____)

5. Here lies _____, tragically assassinated at Ford's Theater.
   (1809–_____)

6. Here lies _____. The teddy bear was named for him.
   (1858–_____)

7. Here lies _____, who became chief justice of the Supreme Court.
   (1857–_____)

8. Here lies _____, who signed the Treaty of Versailles.
   (1856–_____)

9. Here lies _____, unfairly blamed for the Great Depression.
   (1865–_____)

10. Here lies _____. He wrote the New Deal.
    (1882–_____)

11. Here lies _____. He ordered the atomic bombs that ended World War II. (1884–_____)

12. Here lies _____, fatally shot in a Dallas motorcade.
    (1917–_____)

Extended Activity

☆ Research five other presidents. Write possible epitaphs for each of them.

The National Mall

The National Mall is open green space in our nation's capital. It is home to thousands of beautiful trees, flower gardens, pools, and fountains. Close to many of Washington's most famous landmarks, it has become a popular gathering place for many national celebrations and demonstrations.

White House—The White House was the first public building to be built in Washington, D.C. It was constructed in 1792. It has been the home of every American president except for George Washington. The White House was reconstructed after it was destroyed by fire during the War of 1812.

Washington Monument—This monument was erected to honor George Washington. Due to a lack of funding, it took over a century to construct. A group of private citizens finally raised the money for the Washington Monument. It is over 555 feet high, making it the tallest freestanding stone structure in the world.

Vietnam Veterans Memorial—The Vietnam Veterans Memorial was built to honor those soldiers who died or were declared missing during the Vietnam War. Their names are inscribed on the wall. The memorial was designed by a 21-year old student of architecture, Maya Ying Lin. It was built in 1982.

Lincoln Memorial—Outside this memorial, visitors will find 36 columns, which represent the states in the Union at the time of Abraham Lincoln's death in 1865. There are three chambers inside the memorial. Visitors can see a marble statue of Lincoln and read both the Gettysburg Address and Lincoln's second inaugural address.

Korean War Veterans Memorial—Nineteen freestanding granite soldiers honor those men and women who fought in the Korean War. Nearby, visitors can see a wall of faces in the outline of the rugged hills of the Korean landscape.

Thomas Jefferson Memorial—The circular dome of this structure is similar to the one Jefferson used in his personal home, Monticello. The bronze statue of Jefferson was created by Rudolph Evans. Outside the memorial, visitors can see hundreds of Japanese cherry trees.

Franklin Delano Roosevelt Memorial—This monument has four outdoor rooms depicting historical events that occurred during Roosevelt's four terms as president. The memorial contains a statue of the president seated in his wheelchair.

Activity

As a class, create a Washington, D.C., guide book, devoting each page to a different landmark or monument.

Extended Activities

☆ Compare/contrast two or more national monuments on a Venn diagram.

☆ Draw a map of the National Mall. Create a legend with an icon for each monument.

☆ Design a new national monument for the subject or event of your choice.

Packing for the Voyage

In 1620, the Pilgrims crossed the Atlantic Ocean from England to America on the *Mayflower*. The ship carried 102 passengers. Families left their homes and braved the difficult journey, hoping to create a new life for themselves. Space on the ship was limited, so families could take very few personal possessions. They had to leave much of their furniture, animals, books, and toys behind.

Activity

Suppose you were part of a family of four about to cross the Atlantic on the *Mayflower*. Write five personal items each member would take on the voyage. Explain why each would need these items.

Name of Family Member _____
   1. _____
   2. _____
   3. _____
   4. _____
   5. _____
   Reasons_____
   _____

Name of Family Member _____
   1. _____
   2. _____
   3. _____
   4. _____
   5. _____
   Reasons_____
   _____

Name of Family Member _____
   1. _____
   2. _____
   3. _____
   4. _____
   5. _____
   Reasons_____
   _____

Name of Family Member _____
   1. _____
   2. _____
   3. _____
   4. _____
   5. _____
   Reasons_____
   _____

Extended Activity

☆ Pretend you are going to leave your home on a ship in today's world and move to a new land. Space is limited on the ship. Write down five items you would take with you, and why.

Descriptive Language

The use of descriptive language can make an experience come alive for a reader. Good descriptive writers use adjectives to create images that engage the five senses, in order to draw their readers into an experience. For instance, Mark Twain's descriptions of Huckleberry Finn (*The Adventures of Huckleberry Finn,* 1884) floating down the Mississippi on a raft make readers feel that they are right there floating with Huck. Likewise, Sandra Cisneros' descriptions of life on Mango Street (*The House on Mango Street*, 1983) bring readers the tastes, smells, sounds, sights, and feelings of growing up in a big city.

Activity

Choose an American person, place, or thing to describe. First, write down five adjectives to describe your choice. Then fill in sensory details. Finally, write a descriptive paragraph that makes this person, place, or thing come alive for the reader.

My topic: _____

Adjectives to describe topic:

1. _____
2. _____
3. _____
4. _____
5. _____

What my topic smells like: _____

What my topic tastes like: _____

What my topic feels like: _____

What my topic sounds like: _____

What my topic looks like: _____

My Descriptive Paragraph

_____

_____

_____

_____

_____

Extended Activity

☆ Write a descriptive paragraph about a school location without mentioning its name. Then read your paragraph out loud to your classmates and see if they can guess what you are describing!

Crazy Stories

Parts of speech refer to those words that perform different functions in a sentence. Study the chart below to remind yourself of some of the most common parts of speech.

Noun—person, place, or thing. (Example: *Thomas Jefferson* played the *violin*.)

Verb—shows an action of some sort. (Example: These days, Jimmy Carter *builds* houses for poor people.)

Adjective—describes a person, place or thing. (Example: Abraham Lincoln was a *tall*, *thin* man.)

Adverb—describes an adjective, verb, or another adverb. (Example: Former president George Bush *gladly* voted for his son in the presidential election of 2000.)

═══ Activity ═══

Choose a partner. One of you should have a copy of the story below. Don't show the story to your partner. Ask your partner to give you an example of each part of speech asked for under the blank, and write his/her answer in the blank. When you have filled all the blanks, read your crazy story to your partner. Then listen to the stories written by the rest of your classmates.

A Crazy Story about a Future President

Once, there was a _____ named Billy. All his life, he dreamed of being the
                                (noun)

_____ of the United States. In school, he _____ hard.
        (noun)   (verb)

Sometimes, he stayed awake until midnight _____ completing his homework.
                                                            (adverb)

On the weekends, he _____ books about American presidents when he wasn't
                                    (verb)

busy _____ the lawn and babysitting his little _____. He
            (verb)   (noun)

_____ visited _____ museums on the weekends and learned all
        (adverb)   (adjective)

he could about _____. Billy would certainly make a _____
                        (noun)   (adjective)

leader of our country.

═══ Extended Activity ═══

☆ Make up your own story about America. Then erase three nouns, three verbs, three adjectives, and two adverbs. Ask your partner for examples of these parts of speech and fill in the erased portions of your story with his/her suggestions. Then read your crazy story.

Daily Writing Topics

Students may wish to write on the topics below in their journals.

So You Want to be President? and *Eyewitness: Presidents*

1. Do you know someone who would make a good president? Explain.
2. Who do you think was the best president? Explain.
3. Who do you think was the worst president? Explain.
4. What might a president do in his leisure time?
5. What is the president's most important duty? Explain.
6. What are the constitutional requirements for president? Are they adequate or should there be additional requirements? Explain.
7. Which presidents have been assassinated? Choose one and explain the circumstances of the assassination.
8. What career would best prepare someone to be president? Explain.
9. Do you believe a woman or member of a minority will ever be elected president? Why? Why not?
10. Explain how a president can be removed from office.

Uncle Sam and Old Glory

1. Choose one symbol of America and explain its importance to you and your family.
2. Describe three symbols of your community or personal life.
3. Make a list of three American symbols not mentioned in this book. Explain your choices.
4. What does "patriotism" mean to you?
5. What is the meaning of the phrase "E Pluribus Unum"?
6. Benjamin Franklin thought our national symbol should be the turkey instead of an eagle. Do you think a bird other than the eagle would have made a better national symbol? Why? Why not?
7. Explain how and why the Statue of Liberty was given to the United States.
8. Imagine you have been asked to design a new flag to represent the Unites States. What would you design, and why?
9. What was life like for the passengers on board the *Mayflower*? Would you have wanted to be a Pilgrim? Explain.
10. Who was the first Uncle Sam? Why did he become a U.S. symbol?

A is for America

1. How does the American belief in democracy affect people around the world?
2. Compare/contrast a state that has four very different seasons with one where the weather is almost always the same.
3. Explain what manufactured goods/natural resources come from your state.
4. Make a list of birds, flowers, trees, and animals that are native to your state.
5. Explain the contributions of Henry Ford, Thomas Edison, and Margaret Mead.
6. How did the invention of the airplane change life in America?
7. Using the letters that spell "America," think of seven words to describe the United States—beginning with a word that starts with A, then with a word that starts with M, and so on.
8. List all the monuments, memorials, national parks, landmarks, and cities in the state of your choice.
9. Explain Rosa Parks' contribution to the civil rights movement.
10. Describe an appropriate way to celebrate Veterans' Day or Labor Day.

Ode to America

An ode is a type of poem written to honor something or someone. It typically has more than one stanza. Each stanza has four lines that may rhyme in different ways. The last words of the first and third lines or second and fourth lines should rhyme. Below, read this example of an ode:

An Ode to Old Glory

The flag flies high	We pledge allegiance,
For all to see	Honor to
A symbol of	The stars and stripes
Democracy.	And union blue.
Beneath the flag	So stand erect
We all unite	With head held high
Loyal to	When our Old Glory
The cause that's right.	Passes by.

Activity

Write an ode. You may choose to write about a president, state, city, national symbol, or landmark. Use the lines below to list descriptive words or rhyming words that you might use in your poem. On a separate piece of paper, write an ode using your list of ideas. Add a patriotic border to your finished poem.

_____

_____

_____

_____

_____

_____

Extended Activity

☆ In groups of three or four, write an ode to someone at your school. This could be a teacher, custodian, principal, or other helpful person. Give this person a copy of your ode.

Fun with Frybread

Frybread was a main staple made by Native American women on early reservations in the United States. Using government rations, they made this bread and stuffed it with meat for tacos or with berry pudding for dessert. Each cook formed her bread into a particular shape; the shape of the bread affects how it cooks. Contemporary Native Americans fill their frybread with meat, fish, fruit, or jam. Sometimes, they eat it with honey and powdered sugar.

Activity

The following recipe makes four rounds of bread. Study it, and then answer the questions below.

Ingredients

- 1 cup (240 ml) flour
- ½ tablespoon (7.5 ml) baking powder
- ½ teaspoon (2.5 ml) salt
- ½ cup (120 ml) milk
- canola oil heated in a frypan or electric skillet

Directions

Sift dry ingredients. Lightly stir in milk. Add more flour as necessary to make a workable dough. Knead the dough on a floured board with floured hands until smooth. Pinch off fist-sized balls and let students shape them each into a disk. Fry in oil heated to about 375° F (190° C) until golden and done on both sides (about 5 minutes). Drain on absorbent paper and serve with jam or honey and powdered sugar on top.

1. Katie wants to make enough frybread for eight students to each have a round. How much milk will she need?	2. Esperanza would like to make frybread for her Thanksgiving celebration with her nine relatives. To make enough rounds for each guest (including herself), how much flour will she need?
3. Thomas isn't sure if he has enough baking powder for 20 rounds of frybread, one for each of his classmates. How much baking powder will he need?	4. Mario wants to make only one round of frybread. How much milk will he need?

Extended Activity

☆ Figure out the measurements needed to make enough frybread for every person in your class. Adjust the recipe, cook, and enjoy!

Your Average President

You can figure out the average age at inauguration, number of children, years in office, and age at death of presidents by adding the totals in each category, then dividing by the number of presidents you are studying. For instance, if George Washington had two children, Thomas Jefferson had three, and Abraham Lincoln had four, you can figure out the average number of these presidents' children by adding two, three, and four. Then divide this number—nine children—by the number of the presidents you're studying—three. The average number of children among these three presidents was three.

Activity

Use *Eyewitness: Presidents* to complete the chart and compute the averages.

President	Age at Inauguration	Number of Children	Years in Office	Age at Death
George Washington	57	2	8	
Thomas Jefferson		3	8	
Abraham Lincoln		4		56
Zachary Taylor	64	6		65
Franklin Roosevelt	51		12	63
Totals				
Averages				

Extended Activity

☆ Work with a partner to create a chart like the above for five presidents of your choice. Do not use the presidents from the previous list.

President	Age at Inauguration	Number of Children	Years in Office	Age at Death
Totals				
Averages				

Nifty Fifty

Different states were admitted to the Union at different times. New Jersey, Delaware, and Pennsylvania were among the first states to be admitted to the Union. Alaska and Hawaii were the last states to be admitted. Our contemporary American flag has 50 stars on it—one for each of the 50 United States.

Activity

This list shows the date each state was admitted to the Union.

On a separate sheet of paper, put the list in sequential order (1–50).

Alabama—Dec. 14, 1819
Alaska—Jan. 3, 1959
Arizona—Feb. 14, 1912
Arkansas—June 15, 1836
California—Sept. 9, 1850
Colorado—Aug. 1, 1876
Connecticut—Jan. 9, 1788
Delaware—Dec. 7, 1787
Florida—March 3, 1845
Georgia—Jan. 2, 1788
Hawaii—Aug. 21, 1959
Idaho—July 3, 1890
Illinois—Dec. 3, 1818
Indiana—Dec. 28, 1816
Iowa—Dec. 28, 1846
Kansas—Jan. 29, 1861
Kentucky—June 1, 1792
Louisiana—April 30, 1812
Maine—March 15, 1820
Maryland—April 28, 1788
Massachusetts—Feb. 6, 1788
Michigan—Jan. 26, 1837
Minnesota—May 11, 1858
Mississippi—Dec. 10, 1817
Missouri—Aug. 10, 1821

Montana—Nov. 8, 1889
Nebraska—March 1, 1867
Nevada—Oct. 31, 1864
New Hampshire—June 21, 1788
New Jersey—Dec. 18, 1787
New Mexico—Jan. 6, 1912
New York—July 26, 1788
North Carolina—Nov. 21, 1789
North Dakota—Nov. 2, 1889
Ohio—March 1, 1803
Oklahoma—Nov. 16, 1907
Oregon—Feb. 14, 1859
Pennsylvania—Dec. 12, 1787
Rhode Island—May 29, 1790
South Carolina—May 23, 1788
South Dakota—Nov. 2, 1889
Tennessee—June 1, 1796
Texas—Dec. 29, 1845
Utah—Jan. 4, 1896
Vermont—March 4, 1791
Virginia—June 25, 1788
Washington—Nov. 11, 1889
West Virginia—June 20, 1863
Wisconsin—May 29, 1848
Wyoming—July 10, 1890

To the teacher: Students may work in groups for this assignment if you prefer, or you may prepare it as a center activity. Print the state names and dates on individual cards with the number showing their order of admission to the United States on the back. Students can arrange the state cards in order, using the back numbers if they need assistance.

Extended Activity

☆ The U.S. Mint is busy making 50 new state quarters. A new one comes out every ten weeks from 1999 to 2008. The quarters are being released in the same order that the states joined the union. Each state quarter has a design honoring something special about its history or traditions. Many people have been asked to suggest designs for their state quarters. Draw your ideas on a separate sheet of paper for the state quarter of your choice.

The Money Makers: U.S. Mint

The U.S. Mint was created by Congress to produce and distribute coins. Some coins are sold uncirculated, which means they have never been used by anyone. The mint protects the country's $100 billion assets in gold and silver. It has the responsibility for destroying old or damaged coins. The U.S. Mint headquarters is located in Washington, D.C. These presidents are pictured on U.S. coins:

penny (1¢) nickel (5¢) dime (10¢) quarter (25¢) half-dollar (50¢)

Abraham Lincoln Thomas Jefferson Franklin Roosevelt George Washington John Kennedy

Activity

Play this game with a partner. You will need dice and the chart below.

Roll the one die and record your roll number in the left section of any block in the chart. Continue until all blocks have a roll number in them. Then determine the value of each coin and multiply that number by the roll number. Record the value number in the right section of each block. The first two have been done for you. Add all the values to find your total. The player with the highest total is the winner. Play three rounds.

	Lincoln	Jefferson	Roosevelt	Washington	Kennedy	Total
1.	roll 6 / 6¢ / value	roll 4 / 20¢ / value	roll / value	roll / value	roll / value	
2.	roll / value	roll / value	roll / value	roll / value	roll / value	
3.	roll / value	roll / value	roll / value	roll / value	roll / value	

Extended Activity

☆ Place coins under white copy paper. Rub red and blue colored pencils over the coins to reveal the faces of presidents. You may want to use more than one type of each coin and arrange them in creative patterns.

Colonial Comparisons

State population refers to the number of people living in that state. Every ten years, government officials count how many people are living in each state. They use this information to fund public programs and to determine how many representatives each state requires in Congress. The area of a state refers to how large it is. Alaska is the largest state in the nation, with 615,240 square miles. Rhode Island is the smallest state, with only 1,231 square miles.

Activity

Study the population and area totals for the thirteen original colonies. Rewrite the information as two lists in order from the lowest population and area to the highest.

States	Area (in square miles)	Population
Connecticut	5,544	3,405,565
Delaware	2,489	783,600
Georgia	59,441	8,186,453
Maryland	12,407	5,296,486
Massachusetts	10,555	6,349,097
New Hampshire	9,351	1,235,786
New Jersey	8,722	8,414,350
New York	54,475	18,976,457
North Carolina	53,821	8,049,313
Pennsylvania	46,058	12,281,054
Rhode Island	1,545	1,048,319
South Carolina	32,007	4,012,012
Virginia	42,769	7,078,515

Area	Population
1. _____	1. _____
2. _____	2. _____
3. _____	3. _____
4. _____	4. _____
5. _____	5. _____
6. _____	6. _____
7. _____	7. _____
8. _____	8. _____
9. _____	9. _____
10. _____	10. _____
11. _____	11. _____
12. _____	12. _____
13. _____	13. _____

Extended Activity

☆ Use an encyclopedia or the Internet to find out how many representatives your state gets in Congress.

Washington, D.C., Logic Puzzle

There are many historic monuments and buildings to visit in Washington, D.C. Museums, historical buildings, and galleries abound! Visitors could spend a week in this city and still not see all that it has to offer.

Activity

Five friends—José, John, Mary, Thuy, and Yolanda—went on their class trip to Washington, D.C. Each student wanted to visit a different building. Read the clues and fill out the chart to discover which student went where.

Solve this logic puzzle by using the following information. Place an **X** in the box to match each student to the building he or she visited.

1. José stopped by to visit, but the first family wasn't home.
2. John was more interested in current politics than history.
3. Mary climbed 56 steps to stand at the feet of a statue of an assassinated president.
4. Thuy got a cramp in her neck from staring up at this tall memorial.
5. Yolanda loved the Japanese cherry trees outside this domed building.

	White House	Lincoln Memorial	Capitol Building	Jefferson Memorial	Washington Monument
José					
John					
Mary					
Thuy					
Yolanda					

Bald Eagle

Adult bald eagles have dark brown bodies. Their heads, necks, and tails are white. Their beaks and feet are yellow. Weighing between ten to fourteen pounds, they are the second largest birds of prey in the United States, after the California condors. They have hooked beaks and long talons designed for hunting. Bald eagles pierce their prey with their talons, then tear it apart using their strong beaks.

In 1940, the Bald Eagle Protection Act was passed to help the eagles that were being threatened by hunters, loss of habitat, poisoned food supply, and chemical pesticides. During the 1960s and early '70s, bald eagles were placed on the endangered species list. State and federal agencies worked to let people know about their predicament. Land was set aside to protect eagles so that they could breed safely. The species is no longer endangered, but it continues to be threatened. We can lessen harm to bald eagles and other birds by taking down barbed-wire fences, leaving forests uncut for the birds, and reducing our use of pesticides. As raptors, or birds of prey, bald eagles are at the top of the food chain. This means they eat smaller animals that have eaten a variety of smaller animals or plants. If we dump toxic waste into a river and poison fish, then bald eagles who eat the fish are also poisoned.

Activity

Complete the chart showing the effects of chemical pesticides on eagles and their eggs or offspring. Write one effect in each circle.

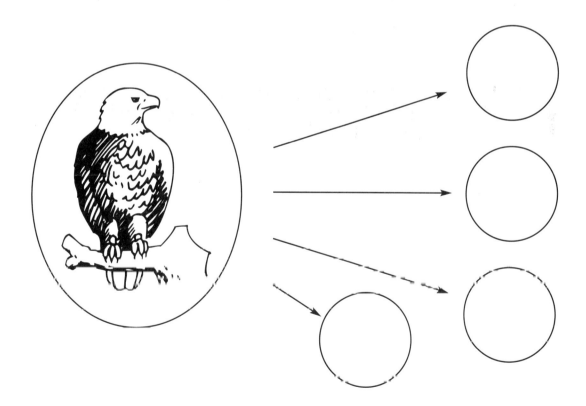

Extended Activities

☆ List five ways humans have harmed the bald eagle population.

☆ Do further research on bald eagles in encyclopedias, books, or on the Internet. Write ten scientific facts about bald eagles.

Buffalo

A full-grown male American buffalo can weigh up to 2,000 pounds and stand six feet tall. They have large horns and a shoulder hump in which they store fat for energy. Buffalo, whose scientific name is bison, are covered with shaggy brown hair. Bison were critical for the survival of the Plains tribes of Native Americans who used them for food, clothing, and shelter.

In 1894, there were only twenty American buffalo in Yellowstone National Park. Congress passed a law to protect them, but in 1902, their population had only grown to 23 in Yellowstone. William Hornaday, a scientist at the New York Zoo, began working to rebuild the herd. As a result of his work, there are now more than 2,000 buffalo living in Yellowstone.

Bison are grazers. They eat their fill, then rest several times during the day. Bison eat approximately 24 pounds of food every day. Their food is mostly grass, mixed with small amounts of forbs and browse. Grass refers to any plant with long, narrow leaves. Forbs are broad-leafed plants like weeds or wildflowers. Browse includes plants with woody stems or thin bark.

Bison belong to a class of animals known as ruminants. They eat and digest their food in a special way. They use their tongues and lower teeth to clip off plants, which they swallow whole. Bison stomachs have four separate parts, which help them digest food. First, food goes to the rumen, then it moves to the reticulum where it is broken down by stomach juices and bacteria and formed into cud. When the bison rests, the cud is pushed back into its mouth where it is mixed with saliva and swallowed again. This time it passes to the third part of the stomach, the omasum, where it is further digested before moving to the fourth part of the stomach, the abomasum. From the abomasum, waste material moves into the bison's intestines and out of its body.

Activities

Make a list of other ruminant animals. Draw a diagram of a ruminant stomach and show the path that food takes.

Complete chart showing the ways in which the Plains Native American tribes used buffalo.

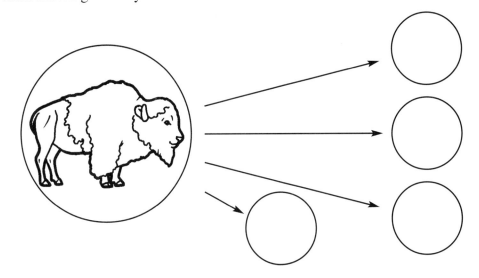

Extended Activities

☆ Find out further details about the American buffalo in encyclopedias, books, or the Internet. Write down ten additional facts.

☆ Research and report on the work that has been done to save the American buffalo from extinction.

Fire Prevention

An artist named Albert Staehle created the cartoon version of Smokey the Bear in 1944. Smokey symbolizes the importance of preventing forest fires. "Only you can prevent forest fires," he says.

A huge forest fire raged in the New Mexico forest in May of 1950, destroying 17,000 acres. A little black bear cub found himself surrounded by flames. He climbed up a burnt tree to escape getting killed. It was here that firefighters found the badly burned and hungry cub. They admired him for his courage and will to survive. They couldn't find his mother, so the firefighters sent the bear cub, Smokey, to live at the National Zoo in Washington, D.C. He was eventually called Smokey Bear after the poster created five years earlier. More than half of these fires are caused by humans. There are over 700 million acres of forests in the United States. These forests provide shade, food, and shelter for wildlife. They also produce oxygen, which we all must have to breathe.

People should never play with fire. A cigarette butt or a spark from a match or a lightning strike can cause dead leaves or branches to burst into flames. Careless people start about half of all forest fires. The trees burned in these fires take decades to grow back.

Here are directions for building a safe campfire:

- Dig a pit away from low tree branches.
- Clear a five-foot area in the dirt around the pit and make a circle of rocks.
- Gather some dry wood and bank it in the center of the pit.

- Ask an adult to strike the match.
- After lighting the fire, put the spent match in water.
- Keep a bucket of water and a shovel nearby.

Activity

Write three rules to remember about fire safety.

1. _____

2. _____

3. _____

Extended Activity

☆ Research a past fire in your area or state. What was the cause of this fire? How many acres burned? What did the fire destroy? Have the plants, animals, and people recovered from this fire?

Be a Washington Meteorologist

Weather is the state of the atmosphere in a particular time and place. Characteristics of weather include temperature, humidity, cloudiness, wind, air pressure, and precipitation. Meteorology is the study of weather and weather forecasting.

══ Activity ══

Find the weather page in your local newspaper. Locate Washington, D.C. Now use this information to answer questions about current weather conditions in our nation's capital.

Date _____

Current Temperature _____

Wind Speed _____

Conditions _____

What kind of weather is predicted for Washington, D.C., during the next two days?

I. Date _____

    High/Low Temperatures _____

    Weather Conditions _____

II. Date _____

    High/Low Temperatures _____

    Weather Conditions _____

Think of two ways the president might be affected by these weather conditions.

_____

_____

_____

_____

══ Extended Activity ══

☆ Use the weather page to locate the weather conditions for your own city. Compare your weather to the weather in Washington, D.C. How might your own weather conditions affect you?

Presidential Birthplace Map

Some presidents, such as John F. Kennedy, grew up in big houses with plenty of money. Other presidents, such as Abraham Lincoln, were born in log cabins to families with little money. Many presidents were born in the Midwest or in the Eastern part of the United States. Only one was born on the West Coast. The 43 American presidents were born in 21 of the 50 states or in colonies that later became states. Here are their birth states:

George Washington—Virginia	**Grover Cleveland**—New Jersey
John Adams—Massachusetts	**Benjamin Harrison**—Ohio
Thomas Jefferson—Virginia	**William McKinley**—Ohio
James Madison—Virginia	**Theodore Roosevelt**—New York
James Monroe—Virginia	**William Taft**—Ohio
John Quincy Adams—Massachusetts	**Woodrow Wilson**—Virginia
Andrew Jackson—South Carolina	**Warren G. Harding**—Ohio
Martin Van Buren—New York	**Calvin Coolidge**—Vermont
William H. Harrison—Virginia	**Herbert C. Hoover**—Iowa
John Tyler—Virginia	**Franklin D. Roosevelt**—New York
James K. Polk—North Carolina	**Harry S. Truman**—Missouri
Zachary Taylor—Virginia	**Dwight D. Eisenhower**—Texas
Millard Fillmore—New York	**John F. Kennedy**—Massachusetts
Franklin Pierce—New Hampshire	**Lyndon B. Johnson**—Texas
James Buchanan—Pennsylvania	**Richard M. Nixon**—California
Abraham Lincoln—Kentucky	**Gerald R. Ford**—Nebraska
Andrew Johnson—North Carolina	**James (Jimmy) Carter**—Georgia
Ulysses S. Grant—Ohio	**Ronald Reagan**—Illinois
Rutherford B. Hayes—Ohio	**George H. W. Bush**—Massachusetts
James Garfield—Ohio	**Bill Clinton**—Arkansas
Chester A. Arthur—Vermont	**George W. Bush**—Connecticut

Activity

Gather together a copy of the blank United States map on page 74 and a set of colored pencils. Use the list above to tally the number of presidents born in each state. Create a map legend using one color to show each different number of presidents that were born in each state—for instance, seven presidents were born in Ohio, so you might choose to color orange every state in which seven presidents were born. Finally, color in your map to correspond with the legend.

Branches of Government

Delegates to the Constitutional Convention knew that a strong central government was important, but they did not want to give any one person too much control. They planned a government with three separate branches called **Legislative**, **Executive**, and **Judicial**. Each branch must work with the other to make the country run smoothly.

The **Legislative** branch is made up of Congress and the government agencies that help them. The Constitution gives Congress the power to make laws. Congress has two parts: the House of Representatives and the Senate.

The **Executive** branch makes sure that the laws of the United States are obeyed. The president is the head of the Executive branch. He gets help and advice from the vice president and Cabinet members. The Constitution states that the president is commander-in-chief of the military.

The **Judicial** branch is made up of the court system. The Supreme Court is the highest court in the land. Courts make decisions about the meaning of laws and how they are applied.

Activity

Complete this chart by labeling the branches of government:

Extended Activity

☆ Each branch of government may use its power to change or challenge the acts of another branch. This plan keeps a balance of power in the government. This is called *checks and balances*. Using an encyclopedia or the Internet, explain how the president uses veto power to change or challenge new laws.

Flag Gallery and History

The United States flag is red, white, and blue. Red signifies hardiness and valor. White symbolizes purity and innocence. Blue stands for vigilance, perseverance, and justice. There are thirteen stripes— seven red and six white—representing the original thirteen colonies. Every time a new state was added to the union, a star was added to the flag. Today's flag has fifty stars on a field of blue. Throughout history, only the number and placement of the stars has changed. Here are pictures of interesting historic flags.

1776—The **Grand Union flag** shows the colonies' allegiance to England (with the Union Jack) and their independence with the stripes.

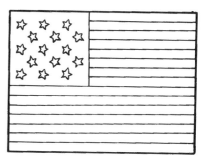

1795—The **Fifteen-star American flag** is the only one with fifteen stripes. It is the flag that Francis Scott Key saw at Ft. McHenry when he wrote "The Star-Spangled Banner."

The **Centennial flag** of 1876 has thirteen red and white stripes with 80 five-pointed stars arranged in the form of the dates "1776" and "1876."

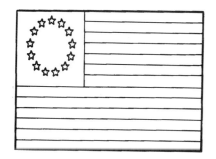

1777—The **Betsy Ross flag** features thirteen five-pointed stars arranged in a circle.

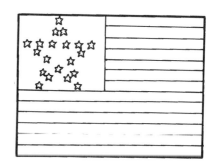

Capt. Samuel C. Reid, a naval hero of the War of 1812, first designed a **Great Star flag** with the stars arranged into one large star pattern. It became a common design during the 19th century.

Extended Activity

☆ Look up a flag from another country. What does it look like compared to the American flag? What do the shapes and colors of that country's flag symbolize?

National Historic Landmarks

To become a National Historic Landmark, a site must be a location in which important historical events occurred, have been the home or work place of a prominent American, or be an outstanding example of architectural design or construction.

These landmarks may be owned by individuals, groups of citizens, or government agencies. The owners are free to manage their property as they choose and may be able to obtain federal funds for restoration and maintenance. Owners are given a bronze nameplate explaining the significance of the landmark. They display this nameplate on their property. Washington, D.C., contains many National Historic Landmarks. Here are just a few:

- **The United States Capitol** houses the meeting chambers of the Senate and the House of Representatives.
- **The Library of Congress** has 22 reading rooms and more than 100 million items in its collection, making it one of the world's leading cultural institutions. It occupies three massive buildings on Capitol Hill.
- *The Philadelphia* is the only surviving gunboat built and manned by American Forces during the Revolutionary War. It is part of the collection at the Smithsonian Institution.

Activity

Write one sentence describing each of the Washington, D.C., landmarks below.

The White House _____

_____

The Smithsonian Institution _____

_____

Marine Corps War Memorial _____

_____

Holocaust Museum _____

_____

Use an encyclopedia or the Internet to find the name and location of three landmarks in each category.

Site of an important historic event	Home of a famous American	Example of significant architectural design or construction
1. _____	1. _____	1. _____
2. _____	2. _____	2. _____
3. _____	3. _____	3. _____

Extended Activity

☆ Locate a landmark in your own community. Describe it in a paragraph. What does it look like, and what is its significance? Draw a picture of the landmark below your paragraph.

National Parks Locator

The United States has many national parks that are protected by the government. The government makes sure that people don't build, hunt, log, or mine in these parks so that people may observe the land in its natural state.

In 1864, President Abraham Lincoln signed an agreement preserving the Yosemite Valley in California for public recreation. Yellowstone National Park became the first official national park in 1872, when President Ulysses S. Grant signed the Yellowstone Act. During the 1890s, three more areas of wilderness became national parks. These include Yosemite, Sequoia, and Mt. Rainier National Parks.

In 1916, Congress established a National Park Service. This is a branch of the Department of the Interior. It is responsible for taking care of these wilderness areas. National parks may be threatened by a variety of problems. Some of these include fires, too much traffic, people who trample delicate plants and poach animals and birds, erosion, and lack of money for upkeep of these important lands.

Activity

Label the following national parks on a copy of the map from page 74.

Arcadia
(Maine)

Carlsbad Caverns
(New Mexico)

Denali
(Alaska)

Everglades
(Florida)

Glacier
(Montana)

Grand Canyon
(Arizona)

Great Smoky Mountains
(Tennessee)

Isle Royale
(Michigan)

Mesa Verde
(Colorado)

Mt. Rainier
(Washington state)

Yellowstone (Idaho, Montana, Wyoming)

Yosemite
(California)

Extended Activities

☆ Design a travel brochure with pictures and information about a national park you have visited or would like to visit.

☆ Make a list of ten more national parks or historic landmarks or monuments. Label them on the map.

Current Events Summary

Here are some examples of ways to summarize current events.

☆ The first continuously published American newspaper was the *Boston News-Letter*, started in 1704 by John Campbell. It contained financial and foreign news, as well as stories about births, deaths, and social events.

☆ The Italian electrical engineer and inventor, Guglielmo Marconi, is credited with having invented the first radio in 1895. Early radio receivers were large and bulky—enormous compared to the tiny radios on which we can listen to the news today.

☆ The first home television receiver was demonstrated in New York in 1928 by the American inventor Ernst F. W. Alexanderson. The first regular television broadcasts began in America in 1939, but after that, they were suspended for two years until just after the war in 1945.

Activity

Listen carefully to a story on a television or radio news broadcast or read an article in the newspaper. Then complete this form.

Date _____   Station _____

Television   Radio   Newspaper   (circle one)

News Anchor(s) or Staff Writer _____

Local   National   International   (circle one)

Answer these questions about the story:

Where does it take place? _____

Who are the most important people in the story? _____

What is the problem? _____

What is being done to solve the problem?_____

Whom does this story affect? Your family? Your community? A foreign country? Explain. _____

_____

If you prefer, you may attach a newspaper article with a major, national news story to this paper. Read the article and complete the summary.

Extended Activity

☆ Compare the same story in two different newspapers—one from America and one from another country. Write a paragraph about how the two stories are the same and how they are different.

64

Veterans' Day

Forty-eight million Americans have served in the military since 1776.

Veterans' Day was created to honor the contributions of military men and women. It is observed on November 11. It was originally called Armistice Day to mark the end of World War I. Because there have been other wars since that time, the name was changed to Veterans' Day to include all those who have served. Many cities have parades and graveside ceremonies to honor the soldiers. The national ceremony for Veterans' Day is held at the Tomb of the Unknown Soldier in Arlington Cemetery. At 11 A.M. on November 11, a color guard of all military branches "presents arms" at the tomb. The president then lays a wreath to honor those who have died.

Branches of the United States Military include the Army, Air Force, Navy, Marines, and Coast Guard. These soldiers serve on the land, in the air, and in the water to protect and defend American freedom.

Activity

Interview a veteran, then fill out the report below.

Name _____

Branch of the U.S. military in which he/she served _____

Rank _____

War(s) fought in _____

Most interesting _____

_____

_____

Bonus Question: What could you do or say to thank this veteran for defending America?

_____

_____

Note to Teacher: You may want to invite a veteran to your classroom to give a talk.

Extended Activity

☆ Below are the official Web sites of the branches of the U.S. military. Research one and write a brief report on how it protects American freedom.

Air Force—*http://www.af.mil/*   **Marines**—*http://www.usmc.mil/*

Army—*http://www.army.mil/*   **Coast Guard**—*http://www.uscg.mil/*

Navy—*http://www.navy.mil/*

All Around Town

After the terrorist attacks of September 11, 2001, displays of American patriotism could be found all over the United States. Flags flew from car antennas and on poles outside people's stores and homes. Americans wore red, white, and blue clothes that were often printed with the phrase, "United We Stand." Such patriotic displays indicate a love of one's country and a belief in that country's ideals and goals.

━━━ Activity ━━━

Look around your hometown for displays of patriotism. Then complete the list below.

Monuments or Memorials

Name of Monument or Memorial   Location

1. _____   _____

2. _____   _____

3. _____   _____

Buildings Named for Famous People

Name of Building and Person   Location

1. _____   _____

2. _____   _____

3. _____   _____

Flags Outside Buildings

Name of Building   Location

1. _____   _____

2. _____   _____

3. _____   _____

━━━ Extended Activity ━━━

☆ Design a flag, T-shirt, building, or other object that displays patriotism. Draw it on a separate sheet of paper.

Norman Rockwell

At age 22, Norman Rockwell was asked to create a cover for America's most popular magazine, *The Saturday Evening Post*. His cover was so well liked that he continued working for that magazine another 47 years. His favorite subjects were common people and traditional or historic American settings. His themes were everyday events. Rockwell refused to paint scenes that were ugly or unpleasant, saying, "I paint life as I'd like it to be." In 1977, he was awarded the Presidential Medal of Freedom for his "vivid and affectionate portraits of our country." Rockwell's friendly and funny style is easy to recognize in magazines, advertisements, calendars, and books. He died in 1978.

Activity

Using an encyclopedia, book, or the Internet, look at a picture painted by Norman Rockwell. Design a patriotic postcard or greeting card in the style of Norman Rockwell in the space below. If possible, transfer your design to heavy paper and color it with markers or paint.

Extended Activity

☆ Use encyclopedias, books, or the Internet to research further details about Norman Rockwell's life. Write down five things you learn about him.

John Philip Sousa

The son of a Portuguese immigrant, John Philip Sousa was an American composer born in 1854. He began taking voice, violin, piano, flute, cornet, baritone trombone, and alto horn lessons as a young boy. His first composition, "Moonlight on the Potomac Waltzes," was published in 1872. He joined the armed forces and served as a Marine. Five years after his discharge, Sousa was asked to return to Washington to lead the U.S. Marine Band, a position he held from 1880–1892.

Upon leaving the Marines, he formed his own band of professional musicians. The members were the best in the world at playing their instruments. Sousa's band was the most popular musical act in the world for over 30 years. It was the first American band to tour the world and play to more than one million people. On December 25, 1896, Sousa composed "The Stars and Stripes Forever," the official march of the United States of America. Because of his life-long interest in marching band music, he was known as the "March King."

In 1893, John Philip Sousa asked the J.W. Pepper Co. to build a special tuba with an upright bell—the conical-shaped opening. He felt the softer sound would be better for concert halls. The instrument was a huge success. The instrument was named the *sousaphone*. He died in 1932.

Activity

In the space bellow, draw a diagram and label the parts of one band instrument of your choice. Choose from a piccolo, flute, clarinet, saxophone, tuba, French horn, trumpet, coronet, glockenspiel, bass drum, or sousaphone.

_____
(name of instrument)

Extended Activity

☆ Ask your school's music teacher to share recordings of John Philip Sousa's marches. Listen to a recording and describe the music in a paragraph.

"This Land is Your Land" Mural

American folk singer and guitarist Woody Guthrie (1912–1967) wrote the words to the famous song, "This Land is Your Land." Throughout the Great Depression, he traveled the United States singing for a living. He wrote many songs about poverty, the difficult lives of migrant workers, and his love for America.

Activity

Listen to a recording of "This Land is Your Land." Then, working in groups of four, depict a scene from the song on a torn paper and painted mural.

Materials

large sheet of butcher paper, construction paper scraps, glue sticks, masking tape, paints, pencils

Directions

1. Tape the paper to an open space on a wall, or lay it on the floor.

2. Plan your scene on a sheet of plain paper.

3. Sketch the scene onto the mural, marking the positions of specific items (e.g., cactus, birds, wheat).

4. Two students can paint the background while two tear off small pieces of construction paper. Let the mural dry.

5. Glue the torn pieces to the painted mural.

Extended Activity

☆ Sing and/or study recordings of the patriotic songs below. Music can be found in *We Sing America: Songs of Patriots and Pioneers* by Pamela Conn Beall and Susan Hagen Nipp (Price Stern Sloan, 1987). Lyrics and history can be found in *Patriotic Songs and Symbols* (Teacher Created Materials, 2002)

Patriotic Song List

"The Star-Spangled Banner"	"Anchors Away"
"Yankee Doodle"	"Marines' Hymn"
"The Battle Hymn of the Republic"	"Caissons Go Rolling Along"
"America"	"Columbia, the Gem of the Ocean"
"America the Beautiful"	"Hail to the Chief"
"This Land is Your Land"	"You're a Grand Old Flag"

"The Star-Spangled Banner"

Francis Scott Key wrote "The Star-Spangled Banner" in 1814, as he watched the British bomb Fort McHenry at Baltimore, Maryland. The words of Key's poem were later set to music. On March 3, 1931, President Hoover signed a bill that made the song the national anthem of the United States.

Activity

Read Francis Scott Key's poem, below. On a separate sheet of paper, write the underlined words, then explain your idea of their meanings. Finally, use a dictionary to write down the actual meanings.

Oh, say can you see, by the dawn's early light,
What so proudly we hailed at the twilight's last <u>gleaming</u>?
Whose broad stripes and bright stars, through the <u>perilous</u> fight,
O'er the ramparts we watched, were so gallantly streaming?
And the rockets' red <u>glare</u>, the bombs bursting in air,
Gave proof through the night that our flag was still there.
O say, does that Star-Spangled Banner yet wave
O'er the land of the free and the home of the brave?

On the shore, <u>dimly</u> seen through the mists of the deep,
Where the foe's <u>haughty</u> host in dread silence <u>reposes</u>,
What is that which the breeze, o'er the towering steep,
As it <u>fitfully</u> blows, now conceals, now <u>discloses</u>?
Now it catches the gleam of the morning's first beam,
In full glory reflected now shines on the stream.
'Tis the Star-Spangled Banner! O long may it wave
<u>O'er</u> the land of the free and the home of the brave.

And where is that band who so <u>vauntingly</u> swore
That the <u>havoc</u> of war and the battle's confusion,
A home and a country should leave us no more?
Their blood has wash'd out their foul footsteps' pollution.
<u>Refuge</u> could save the <u>hireling</u> and slave
From the terror of flight or the gloom of the grave:
And the Star-Spangled Banner in triumph doth wave
O'er the land of the free and the home of the brave.

Oh! thus be it ever, when freemen shall stand
Between their loved homes and the war's <u>desolation</u>!
Blest with victory and peace, may the heaven-rescued land
Praise the Power that hath made and <u>preserved</u> us a nation.
Then conquer we must, for our cause it is just,
And this be our <u>motto</u>: "In God is our trust."
And the Star-Spangled Banner forever shall wave
O'er the land of the free and the home of the brave!

Extended Activity

☆ Using an encyclopedia, book, or the Internet, research the history of another patriotic song. Refer to the bottom of page 69 for song ideas.

All American Picnic

Hot Dogs

Hot dogs have long been a favorite American food. Different cities offer different variations on the classic frankfurter. Here are a few variations:

Kansas City Dogs	*Tex Mex Dogs*
Sauerkraut	Salsa
Swiss cheese (melted)	Monterey Jack cheese
Coney Island (Chili Dogs)	Chopped jalapeños
Canned chili without beans	Tortillas
Chicago Dogs	***Vegetarian Dogs***
Relish	Tofu or tempeh hot dog
Mustard	Ketchup
Chopped onion	Mustard
Chopped tomato	Pickle relish
Celery salt	Whole wheat bun

Heat the dogs in a pot of boiling water or roast them on an outdoor grill. Wrap the dogs in buns or tortillas.

Popcorn

Native Americans grew corn (maize) before the first settlers came to America. Follow package directions to make hot air or microwave popcorn. Top with melted butter and salt or grated cheddar cheese. Serve in paper bags.

Apple Pie

Early settlers brought apple seeds to America. Apples were grown in New England as early as 1630. A man named Johnny Appleseed was responsible for extensive plantings of apple orchards in the Midwestern United States.

Bake frozen apple pies. One pie will serve 6–8 students. Cut it into small wedges and serve it with vanilla ice cream or whipped cream.

Beverage

Prepare red and/or blue soft drink mix according to package directions. Chill and serve.

Baseball

Baseball has been America's "national pastime" for almost 150 years. It's a perfect game for a picnic. Remind your students to bring their baseball gloves, bats, and balls. Divide the class into two teams. One team takes the field while the other team is at bat. The team that scores the most runs in nine innings is the winner.

All American Time Capsule

A time capsule is a fun and interesting way to preserve history for future generations. First, select a water-resistant plastic container or metal tin large enough to hold the items you've collected. Then, collect items that are uniquely American. Students may want to include the following:

☆ a picture of the current president

☆ a fast food menu

☆ television schedule

☆ magazine articles

☆ dated newspaper articles

☆ fad items from popular culture

☆ personal photos

☆ video or audio taped interviews or music

☆ a ballgame scorecard or rock concert program

☆ advertisements showing things that will change with time, like automobiles or clothing styles

Wrap all the items in acid-free tissue or plastic bubble wrap. Place them inside the container and seal. Store in a cool, dry place, perhaps in the back of a closet or safe in the school office. Make a note of a date that your capsule should be opened.

Games

Each of these games will work well for identifying proper names. You may use the names of presidents, first ladies, states, capital cities, national landmarks, or national symbols.

Twenty Questions

One player decides on a target name (after first announcing a category) and writes it on a slip of paper. Other players in turn may ask up to 20 questions of him or her in an effort to guess the name. The player who correctly guesses the name on the paper gets to begin the next round.

Guess-a-Sketch

Provide chart paper and a marker or crayons. Write the words "person," "place," or "thing" on separate slips of paper and drop them in a container. The first player selects a paper and draws a sketch of an item that matches his or her category. The first student to call out the name of the item being drawn wins the next turn.

Charades

Prepare slips of paper with the names of presidents, cities, states, monuments, etc., that have been used in this unit. Store them in a closed container. Players in turn select a slip of paper from the container and try to act out the words. They may not speak. The first student to call out the word(s) being acted out wins the next turn.

Flag Ceremony

You may choose to join another class for a flag-raising ceremony and the creation of a time capsule. These activities may be done independently or as part of your all American picnic described on the previous page.

Schools display the flag during business hours near or in front of the school office. If you wish, you may include the entire student body in a ceremony to raise or lower the flag.

Discuss the following rules with your class and observe them during the flag ceremony:

☆ The flag should not be displayed on days when weather conditions could damage it.

☆ The flag should be attached to the ropes and raised to the top of the flagpole.

☆ During the playing (or singing) of the national anthem, all persons should stand at attention facing the flag and with their right hands over their hearts.

☆ The Pledge of Allegiance should be said while standing at attention facing the flag with the right hand over the heart.

☆ "Taps" may be played at the close of the day as the flag is being lowered.

☆ Two students should fold the flag. The flag should never touch the ground. First, it is folded in half, then quarters lengthwise. Next, fold a triangular flap up toward the open end of the fold. Continue folding the flag over and over in a series of triangles until you reach the union blue end. This will work best if one student folds and the other student supports the weight of the flag. Before the last fold, the student who has been holding the flag should open his end so that the final fold can be tucked inside. This will create a neat triangle that cannot easily fall open.

Bulletin Board Ideas

Presidential Birthplace

☆ Use an overhead projector to enlarge the map on page 74. Attach it to a bulletin board. Copy and cut apart the presidents' faces on pages 75 and 76. Connect them to their birth states with a length of yarn.

Monuments

☆ At another time, place monument pictures on the map. Copy and cut out the monument pictures on page 77. Connect the pictures to their locations with a length of yarn.

State Capitals

☆ Print the names of 50 capital cities on 1" x 2" (2.54 cm x 5 cm) lightweight cards for an interactive bulletin board. Attach the city names to the map with push pins.

United States Map

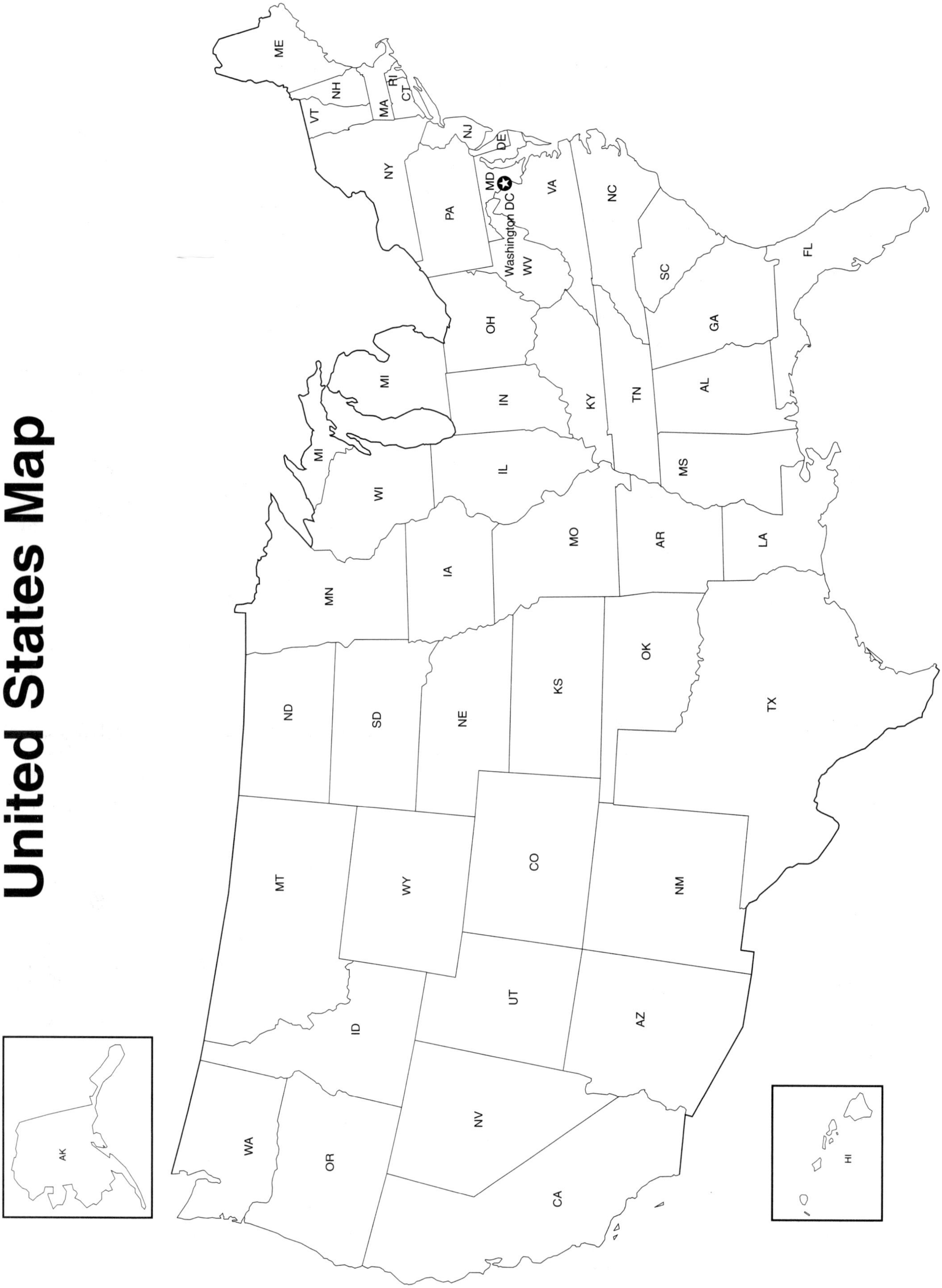

ME

NH

VT

NY

MA

CT

RI

NJ

DE

PA

MD

Washington DC

VA

WV

OH

MI

IN

KY

NC

SC

GA

TN

AL

MS

MI

WI

IL

MO

AR

LA

IA

MN

MO

OK

ND

SD

NE

KS

TX

MT

WY

CO

NM

ID

UT

AZ

NV

WA

OR

CA

AK

HI

Presidents' Faces

George
Washington

John Adams

Thomas
Jefferson

James Madison

James Monroe

John Quincy
Adams

Andrew Jackson

Martin Van Buren

William H.
Harrison

John Tyler

James Polk

Zachary Taylor

Millard Fillmore

Franklin Pierce

James Buchanan

Abraham Lincoln

Andrew Johnson

Ulysses S. Grant

Rutherford B.
Hayes

James A.
Garfield

Chester A. Arthur

Grover
Cleveland

Presidents' Faces *(cont.)*

Benjamin
Harrison

William McKinley

Theodore
Roosevelt

William Howard
Taft

Woodrow Wilson

Warren G.
Harding

Calvin Coolidge

Herbert Hoover

Franklin D.
Roosevelt

Harry S. Truman

Dwight D.
Eisenhower

John F. Kennedy

Lyndon B.
Johnson

Richard M. Nixon

Gerald Ford

Jimmy Carter

Ronald Reagan

George Bush

Bill Clinton

George W. Bush

Our Country Clip Art

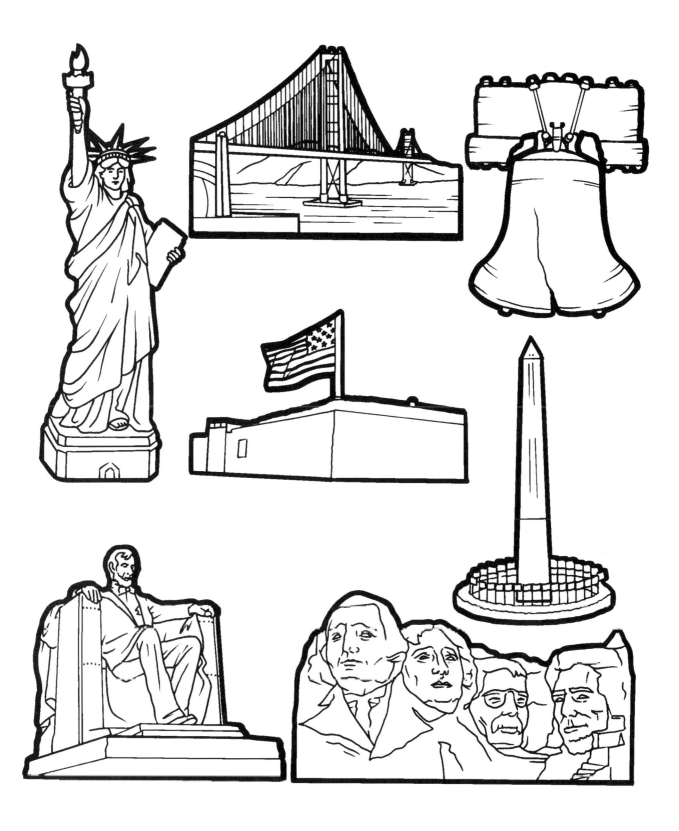

Bibliography

Books

Bausam, Ann. *Our Country's Presidents*. National Geographic, 2001.

Bellamy, Francis. *The Pledge of Allegiance*. Scholastic, 2001.

Blassingame, Wyatt. *The Look-It-Up Book of Presidents*. Random House, 2001.

Cheney, Lynne. *America—A Patriotic Primer*. Simon and Schuster, 2002.

Curlee, Lynn. *Liberty*. Atheneum, 2000.

Davis, Kenneth, C. *Don't Know Much about the 50 States*. Harper Collins, 2001.

Giesecke, Ernestine. *National Government, Kids' Guide Series*. Reed Educational and Professional Publishing, 2000.

Hale, Anna W. *The Mayflower People*. Roberts Rinehart, 1995.

Holzschuher, Cynthia. *U. S. History Brain Teasers*. Teacher Created Materials, 2001.

———. *Focus on Presidents*. Teacher Created Materials, 1997.

Krull, Kathleen. *Lives of the Presidents, Fame, Shame and What the Neighbors Thought*. Harcourt, Brace Jovanovich, 1998.

Pastan, Amy. *First Ladies*. Dorling Kindersley Eyewitness Books, 2001.

Priebe, Mac. *The Bald Eagle*: *Endangered No More*. Mindfull Press, 2000.

Provensen, Alice. *The Buck Stops Here*. Harper Collins, 1990.

Robb, Don. *Hail to the Chief: The American Presidency*. Charlesbridge, 2000.

Ryan, Pam Munoz. *The Flag We Love*. Charlesbridge, 2001.

Sewall, Marcia. *The Pilgrims of Plymouth*. Atheneum, 1986.

Sobel, Syl. *How the U.S. Government Works*. Barrons Juvenile, 1999.

Web Sites

http://www.whitehouse.gov/

http://www.ipl.org/ref/POTUS/

http://www.americanpresidents.org/classroom

http://gi.grolier.com/presidents/

http://www.pbs.org/wgbh/amex/presidents/indexjs.html

http://www.theamericanpresidency.net/

http://www.webpresidentsusa.com/

http://americanhistory.si.edu/presidency/2_frame.html

http://www.geocities.com/CapitolHill/Lobby/5691/etiquette.html (flag)

http://www.greatseal.com/ (Great Seal)

http://www.bcpl.net/~etowner/anthem.html (national anthem)

http://www.baldeagleinfo.com/index.html (bald eagle)

http://www.50states.com/ (states)

http://www.nps.gov/ (National Park Service)

Answer Key

Presidential Name Game—page 8

James
1. Polk
2. Monroe
3. Madison
4. Buchanan
5. Garfield
6. Carter

Andrew
1. Jackson
2. Johnson

John
1. Kennedy
2. Tyler
3. Adams
4. Quincy Adams

George
1. Washington
2. Bush
3. W. Bush

William
1. McKinley
2. Clinton
3. Taft
4. Harrison

Franklin
1. Pierce
2. Roosevelt

Presidential Facts—page 9
1. Bush
2. Taft
3. Roosevelt
4. Reagan
5. Coolidge
6. Harrison
7. Roosevelt
8. Adams
9. Ford
10. Taylor
11. Eisenhower
12. Johnson
13. Clinton
14. Cleveland
15. Harrison
16. Truman
17. Lincoln
18. Washington
19. Nixon
20. Carter

James Buchanan, Grover Cleveland, John Tyler

Mount Rushmore—page 10
1. Washington—Father of Our Country, Constitution, Revolutionary War hero
2. Jefferson—westward expansion, Declaration of Independence
3. Lincoln—anti-slavery, Civil War
4. T. Roosevelt—concern for environment

George Washington—page 12
1. Feb. 22, 1732, Westmoreland County, VA.
2. Martha Custis, John and Martha
3. He was an army general.
4. As president, he led the Constitutional Convention, designed Washington, D.C., and planned our strong democratic government.

Thomas Jefferson—page 13
1. Feb. 1743, Virginia
2. Two daughters
3. He danced, played the violin, and rode horses. He did well in school. He was an excellent writer.
4. The Declaration of Independence

Abraham Lincoln—page 14
1. Feb. 12, 1809, Kentucky
2. Mary Todd, Robert, Edward, William, and Tad
3. Lincoln was against slavery.
4. April 14, 1865, at Ford's Theater, Washington, D.C.

Franklin Delano Roosevelt—page 15
1. Jan. 30, 1882, Hyde Park, NY
2. Eleanor, Franklin Jr., Anna, James, Elliott, John
3. The New Deal created work projects and protected the banking system.
4. FDR was stricken with polio in 1921.

Presidential Patriots—page 16

#	Presidents	Diplomat	Military Leader	Governor	Congress	Vice President
2	John Adams	X			X	X
3	Thomas Jefferson	X		X	X	X
8	Martin Van Buren			X	X	X
13	Millard Fillmore		X		X	X
26	Theodore Roosevelt		X	X		X
28	Woodrow Wilson	X		X		
30	Calvin Coolidge			X	X	X
33	Harry Truman		X		X	X
34	Dwight Eisenhower	X	X			
35	John Kennedy		X		X	
37	Richard Nixon		X		X	X
39	Jimmy Carter	X	X	X	X	

Flag Etiquette—page 20
1. ground
2. flag
3. vertically
4. torn
5. destroyed
6. flag
Old Glory

The Pledge of Allegiance—page 21
1. I pledge allegiance
2. to the Flag
3. of the United States of America
4. and to the Republic for which it stands
5. one nation
6. under God,
7. indivisible,
8. with liberty and justice for all.

The Great Seal—page 23
1. eagle, national bird
2. arrows, symbol of war
3. olive branch, symbol of peace
4. stripes, original colonies
5. shield, strength and protection
6. thirteen, the number of original colonies
7. stars, original colonies
8. "out of many, one" - one nation is made of many states

Timely Dates—page 35
1. 1776
2. 1846
3. 1903
4. 1787
5. 1863
6. 1983
7. 1969
8. 1881
9. 1893
10. 1963
11. 1955
12. 1919
13. 1852
14. 1848
15. 1931

Answer Key *(cont.)*

Latitude and Longitude—page 36

	CITY	STATE	LATITUDE	LONGITUDE
1.	Philadelphia	PA	39.95N	5.16W
2.	Boston	MA	42.36N	71.06W
3.	Chicago	IL	41.85N	87.65W
4.	Cleveland	OH	41.50N	81.7W
5.	Charlotte	NC	35.23N	80.84W
6.	Cincinnati	OH	38.95N	83.86W
7.	New Orleans	LA	29.61N	90.09W
8.	New York City	NY	40.71N	74.01W
9.	Wheeling	WV	40.06N	80.72W
10.	Dover	DE	39.16N	75.52W
11.	Detroit	MI	42.33N	83.05W
12.	Phoenix	AZ	33.45N	112.07W
13.	Tombstone	AZ	31.7N	110.07W
14.	Jamestown	VA	37.21N	76.77W
15.	Dallas	TX	32.78N	96.8W

Presidential Epitaphs—page 42

1. Thomas Jefferson—1826
2. Andrew Jackson—1837
3. William Henry Harrison—1841
4. Zachary Taylor—1850
5. Abraham Lincoln—1865
6. Theodore Roosevelt—1919
7. William Howard Taft—1930
8. Woodrow Wilson—1924
9. Herbert Hoover—1964
10. Franklin Delano Roosevelt—1945
11. Harry Truman—1972
12. John F. Kennedy—1963

Fun with Frybread—page 49

1. 1 cup of milk
2. 2 ½ cups of flour
3. 2 ½ tablespoons of baking powder
4. ⅛ cups of milk

Your Average President—page 50

Washington—67
Jefferson—57, 83
Lincoln—52, 4
Taylor—1
F. Roosevelt—5
Totals/Averages:
Age at Inauguration—281/56.2
Children—20/4
Years in office—33/6.6
Age at Death—334, 66.8

Nifty Fifty—page 51

1. Delaware
2. Pennsylvania
3. New Jersey
4. Georgia
5. Connecticut
6. Massachusetts
7. Maryland
8. South Carolina
9. New Hampshire
10. Virginia
11. New York
12. North Carolina
13. Rhode Island
14. Vermont
15. Kentucky
16. Tennessee
17. Ohio
18. Louisiana
19. Indiana
20. Mississippi
21. Illinois
22. Alabama
23. Maine
24. Missouri
25. Arkansas
26. Michigan
27. Florida
28. Texas
29. Iowa
30. Wisconsin
31. California
32. Minnesota
33. Oregon
34. Kansas
35. West Virginia
36. Nevada
37. Nebraska
38. Colorado
39. North Dakota
40. South Dakota
41. Montana
42. Washington
43. Idaho
44. Wyoming
45. Utah
46. Oklahoma
47. New Mexico
48. Arizona
49. Alaska
50. Hawaii

Colonial Comparisons—page 53

Area:

1.	RI	8.	SC
2.	DE	9.	VA
3.	CT	10.	PA
4.	NJ	11.	NC
5.	NH	12.	NY
6.	MA	13.	GA
7.	MD		

Population:

1.	DE	8.	VA
2.	RI	9.	NC
3.	NH	10.	GA
4.	CT	11.	NJ
5.	SC	12.	PA
6.	MD	13.	NY
7.	MA		

Washington D.C., Logic Puzzle—page 54

José—White House
John—Capitol
Mary—Lincoln Memorial
Thuy—Washington Monument
Yolanda—Jefferson Memorial

Branches of Goverment—page 60

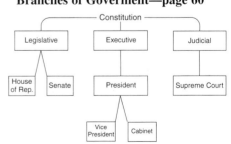